## Books by Steven M. Fiser

The
ABSITE
Review

The *practice* ABSITE
Question
Book

The
Senior ABSITE
Review

The ABS General Surgery
Oral Certifying Exam
Review
(Available 2007)

The practice ABSITE Question Book
(Author of The ABSITE Review)

Steven M. Fiser MD
Hancock Surgical Consultants, LLC
Boston, Massachusetts

# Contents:

## Cell biology

1. Two weeks after a whipple operation, your patient continues to have early satiety with oral intake. You decide to start metoclopramide and erythromycin. What receptor does erythromycin bind to increase gastro-intestinal motility?
   a. Somatostatin receptor
   b. Acetylcholine and dopaminergic receptors
   c. GABA receptor
   d. Motilin receptor

   **Answer: d.** Erythromycin binds the motilin receptor. The motilin receptor is found primarily in the stomach, duodenum, and colon.

   Metoclopramide improves motility by stimulating acetylcholine release and by blocking dopaminergic receptors.

2. Proteins are synthesized from:
   a. mRNA
   b. tRNA
   c. double stranded DNA
   d. single stranded DNA

   **Answer: a.** mRNA is synthesized from DNA by RNA polymerase. mRNA then goes to the cytoplasm and ribosomes read the mRNA and make proteins. tRNA have amino acids bound to them which form proteins after the tRNA attaches to the ribosome binding site.

3. One week after an abdominoperineal resection, your patient develops urosepsis requiring volume resuscitation, antibiotics, and moderate amounts of levophed and vasopressin. E. coli grows out from the blood cultures. What portion of the lipopolysaccharide complex accounts for its toxicity?
   a. Lipid A

    b.   Lipid B
    c.   Lipid C
    d.   Lipid D

**Answer: a.** Lipid A is the toxic portion of the lipopolysaccharide complex found with gram negative sepsis. Lipid A is a very potent stimulant for TNF-alpha release.

4.   Steroid hormones:
    a.   Bind a receptor on the plasma membrane and activate a plasma membrane enzyme
    b.   Bind a cytoplasmic receptor, enter the nucleus, and affect transcription of proteins
    c.   Bind a receptor in the nucleus and affect transcription of proteins
    d.   Do not enter the cell

**Answer b.** Steroid hormones bind a receptor in the cell cytoplasm, enter the nucleus as a steroid- receptor complex, and then affect transcription of proteins.

Thyroid hormone affects transcription after binding a receptor that resides in the nucleus.

5.   Four days after an Ivor Lewis esophagectomy, you decide to start enteral tube feedings through a J-tube. The long chain fatty acids contained in the tube feeds:
    a.   Enter the circulation via the portal system
    b.   Enter the circulation via lymphatics
    c.   Are only synthesized in the body
    d.   Are not found in chylomicrons

**Answer b.** Long chain fatty acids enter the body through terminal lacteals (absorption through the lymphatic system) either as free long chain fatty acids or as chylomicrons.

Medium chain and short chain fatty acids along with proteins and carbohydrates enter through the portal circulation.

6. Cells divide during what phase of the cell cycle?
   a. G1
   b. S
   c. G2
   d. M

**Answer d.** Cells divide during the M phase.

The G1 phase determines cell cycle length (some consider part of this phase to be G0).

S phase is the synthesis phase where proteins are made in preparation for division. Chromosomal duplication also occurs during this phase.

G2 phase is just a space between the S phase and M phase.

M phase is when the cell divides.

7. Of the following, which is the most critical component in the neovascularization of tumor metastases?
   a. HER receptor
   b. VEGF receptor
   c. Neu receptor
   d. FGF receptor

**Answer b.** One of the most critical elements in the neovascularization of metastases is the VEGF (vascular endothelial growth factor) receptor.

Many new chemotherapeutic strategies are targeting the VEGF receptor.

# Hematology

8. For its anti-coagulation effects, heparin binds:
   a. Protein C
   b. Protein S
   c. Anti-thrombin III
   d. Factor VII

   **Answer c.** Heparin binds anti-thrombin III.

   This complex then binds thrombin, factor IX, factor X, and factor XI.

9. Seven days after a kidney transplant, your patient develops severe acute rejection with vasculitis on biopsy. You decide to start the monoclonal antibody OKT3. Monoclonal antibodies:
   a. Bind one epitope at one site
   b. Bind one epitope at multiple sites
   c. Bind multiple epitopes on a single antigen
   d. Bind multiple epitopes on multiple antigens

   **Answer a.** Monoclonal antibodies (such as OKT3) are all identical, so they bind one epitope at the exact same binding site.

10. You start coumadin on a patient with a pulmonary embolus. Three days later, he starts sloughing off skin across his arms and legs. All of the following are true of this patients most likely condition except:
    a. This likely would have been prevented by starting heparin before coumadin
    b. Patients with protein C deficiency are more susceptible to this problem
    c. The skin sloughing is caused by skin necrosis
    d. This is likely due to hemophilia A

**Answer d.** Warfarin induced skin necrosis occurs in patients started on coumadin without being given heparin 1st. It results from a relatively hyper-coaguable state that can occur in some individuals because of the shorter half-life of protein C and S compared to factors II, VII, IX and X. Protein C and S decrease after coumadin before the other factors decrease, resulting in a relatively hypercoaguable state.

Patients with protein C deficiency are at increased risk for this problem, which is prevented by starting heparin before giving coumadin.

11. While performing a low anterior resection for colon cancer in a patient on chronic dialysis, you notice a significant amount of bloody oozing from your dissection plane. All of the following are true of uremic induced platelet dysfunction except:
    a. Down regulates GpIb
    b. Down regulates GpIIb/IIIa
    c. Stimulates von Willebrand's factor release
    d. Treatment of choice is dialysis

**Answer c.**

Uremia down regulates GpIb, GpIIb/IIIa, and vWF.

Dialysis is the initial treatment of choice for uremic coagulopathy.

Other treatment options in this patient include DDAVP and conjugated estrogens which stimulate the release of factor VIII and vWF.

Platelets are also an option.

## Blood products

12. The most common blood transfusion reaction is:
    a. Clerical error leading to ABO incompatibility
    b. Transfusion related acute lung injury
    c. Delayed hemolysis from reaction to minor antigens
    d. Febrile non-hemolytic transfusion reaction

    **Answer d.** (see below)

13. Prevention of febrile non-hemolytic transfusion reaction in patients requiring blood involves:
    a. Heating blood to destroy the white blood cells
    b. Prophylactic antibiotics
    c. NSAID's
    d. Leukocyte filter

    **Answer d.** The most common transfusion reaction is febrile non-hemolytic transfusion reaction which occurs from white blood cells in the donor blood.

    The transfusion reaction can be prevented by using a leukocyte filter during transfusion (the filter size is large enough to allow red blood cells through but small enough to trap white blood cells).

    Clerical error leading to ABO incompatibility is the most common transfusion reaction leading to death.

14. The most common blood product containing bacterial contamination is:
    a. Red blood cells
    b. Platelets
    c. Cryoprecipitate
    d. Fresh frozen plasma

**Answer b.** (see below)

15. The most common bacterial contaminant in blood products is:
    a. Gram positive cocci
    b. Gram negative rods
    c. Anaerobes
    d. Gram positive rods

    **Answer b.** The most common blood product to contain a bacterial contaminant is platelets because they are stored at room temperature which offers a good medium for bacterial growth.

    The most common bacteria found with blood product contamination is gram negative rods (specifically E. coli).

    Platelets last for 5 days stored at room temperature. They are not stored in a cold environment because it significantly decreases their half-life.

## Infection and Antibiotics

16. The most common acquired hospital infection is:
    a. Pneumonia
    b. Blood stream infection
    c. Urinary tract infection
    d. Colitis

    **Answer c.** The most common acquired hospital infection is urinary tract infection. This is often related to placement of urinary catheters. The best treatment of a urinary tract infection is removal of the catheter.

17. The most common cause of bloodstream infection:
    a. Urinary tract infection
    b. Pneumonia
    c. Colitis
    d. Central line sepsis

    **Answer d.** The most common cause of blood stream infection is central line sepsis. When a patient spikes a fever, you need to send off blood, urine, and sputum cultures. Check a CXR to make sure there is not an infiltrate and change all the lines (try to get rid of them altogether if possible). Check the patient's wound and send off a white count.

18. Antibiotics can be subdivided into bacteriostatic and bacteriocidal antibiotics. Each of the following antibiotics is considered bacteriostatic except:
    a. Bactrim
    b. Tetracycline
    c. Erythromycin
    d. Gentamicin

**Answer d.** Bacteriostatic agents include chloramphenicol, tetracycline, clindamycin, erythromycin, and bactrim.

19. The mechanism of aminoglycoside resistance is:
    a. Plasmids for beta-lactamase
    b. Changes in cell wall binding protein
    c. Decreased active transport due to modifying enzymes
    d. Enhanced metabolism of the bacteria

**Answer c.** Active transport of aminoglycosides is decreased by modification of the transport proteins by enzymes.

20. The mechanism of penicillin resistance is:
    a. Plasmids for beta-lactamase
    b. Changes in cell wall binding protein
    c. Decreased active transport due to modifying enzymes
    d. Enhanced metabolism of the bacteria

**Answer a.** The usual mechanism of penicillin resistance is by plasmids coding for beta-lactamase.

The mechanism of vancomycin resistance is changes in cell wall binding protein.

21. Appropriate vancomycin peak and trough values are:
    a. Peak 20-40, trough 5-10
    b. Peak 5-10, trough < 1
    c. Peak 40-80, trough 20-40
    d. Peak < 1, trough 5-10

**Answer a.** The appropriate peak (20-40) and trough (5-10) values for vancomycin are important in patients with renal failure.

22. Appropriate gentamicin peak and trough values are:
    a.  Peak 20-40, trough 5-10
    b.  Peak 5-10, trough < 1
    c.  Peak 40-80, trough 20-40
    d.  Peak < 1, trough 5-10

    **Answer b.** The appropriate peak (5-10) and trough (< 1) values for gentamicin are important in patients with renal failure.

23. A patient on gentamicin has a peak level of 80 and a trough of <1. The most appropriate management is:
    a.  Continue current dosing
    b.  Decrease dose but maintain frequency
    c.  Decrease dose and decrease frequency
    d.  Maintain dose and decrease frequency

    **Answer b.** To decrease the peak level of a drug, one needs to decrease the dose of the drug (the peak level is taken 1 hour after dosing).

    To decrease the trough of a drug, you need to increase the interval at which the drug is given (decrease frequency or longer time between doses).

24. The mechanism of action for fluoroquinolones is:
    a.  Inhibition of RNA polymerases
    b.  Inhibition of DNA gyrase
    c.  Inhibition of ribosomes
    d.  Production of oxygen radicals

    **Answer b.** Fluoroquinolones inhibit DNA gyrase. They are bacteriocidal agents.

13

25. The mechanism of action for metronidazole is:
    a. Inhibition of RNA polymerases
    b. Inhibition of DNA gyrase
    c. Inhibition of ribosomes
    d. Production of oxygen radicals

    **Answer d.** Metronidazole produces oxygen radicals which break up DNA in bacteria. It is a bacteriocidal agent.

26. A patient with an enterococcal blood stream infection is best treated by which of the following antibiotics:
    a. Cefazolin
    b. Ceftriaxone
    c. Bactrim
    d. Ampicillin

    **Answer d.** Ampicillin was specifically designed to treat enterococcus, although this will not pick up VRE (vancomycin resistant enterococcus). The cephalosporins ($1^{st}$, $2^{nd}$, and $3^{rd}$ generation) do not pick up enterococci. Bactrim does not cover enterococci either.

27. Sludging in the gallbladder and cholestatic jaundice is characteristic of which of the following antibiotics:
    a. Quinolones
    b. Bactrim
    c. Erythromycin
    d. Ceftriaxone

    **Answer d.** Sludging in the gallbladder and cholestatic jaundice are complications of ceftriaxone.

28. Erythema multiforme is most likely with which of the following antibiotics:
   a. Quinolones
   b. Bactrim
   c. Erythromycin
   d. Ceftriaxone

   **Answer b.** Bactrim has many side-effects associated with it. These include allergic reactions, renal damage, erythema multiforme, and hemolysis in G6PD deficient patients.

29. Of the following anti-tuberculosis drugs, which is most likely to cause retrobulbar neuritis:
   a. Isoniazide
   b. Rifampin
   c. Pyrazinamide
   d. Ethambutol

   **Answer d.** Retrobulbar neuritis is a complication of ethambutol.

30. Of the following anti-tuberculosis drugs, which is most likely to cause B-6 deficiency:
   a. Isoniazid
   b. Rifampin
   c. Pyrazinamide
   d. Ethambutol

   **Answer a.** Isoniazid therapy is most likely to cause B-6 deficiency.

## Anesthesia

31. Malignant hyperthermia is most commonly is related to a defective receptor (ryanodine receptor) on the sarcoplasmic reticulum that controls calcium release. The 1$^{st}$ sign of malignant hyperthermia after receiving succinylcholine in an intubated patient is:
    a. Fever
    b. Rigors
    c. Increase in end-tidal $CO_2$
    d. Tachycardia

    **Answer c.** (see below)

32. The most appropriate step in the treatment of malignant hyperthermia is:
    a. Dantrolene
    b. Dopamine
    c. Dobutamine
    d. Lasix and potassium

    **Answer a.** Malignant hyperthermia can be triggered by either volatile gaseous inhalation anesthetics (sevoflurane, isoflurane, halothane, enflurane, etc.) or succinylcholine.

    The defect is in calcium metabolism which causes a prolonged muscle excitation-contraction syndrome.

    In an intubated patient, the 1$^{st}$ sign of malignant hyperthermia is a rise in end-tidal $CO_2$.

    Other signs/symptoms include tachycardia, fever, rigidity, acidosis, and hyperkalemia.

    Treatment includes stopping the precipitating anesthetic (or paralytic), dantrolene (which decouples the excitation complex), cooling blankets, $HCO_3-$, glucose, and oxygen.

33. Cis-atracurium is metabolized by:
    a. Liver
    b. Kidney
    c. Plasma cholinesterase
    d. Hoffman degradation

    **Answer d.** Cis-atracurium is degraded by Hoffman degradation which makes it ideal for patients with either renal failure or liver failure.

34. Two days after a severe inhalational injury, you have trouble oxygenating your patient so you decide to paralyze her with pancuronium. The most common side effect of pancuronium is:
    a. Fever
    b. Hypotension
    c. Increased intracranial pressure
    d. Tachycardia

    **Answer d.** The most common side effect of pancuronium (non-depolarizing muscle relaxant) is tachycardia.

35. A 52 yo woman undergoes a routine low anterior resection for colon cancer and has a temperature of 104.0 six hours post-op. You look at her wound and it looks purple around the edges and there seems to be some gray drainage. The most appropriate next step in management is:
    a. Cefazolin
    b. Ceftriaxone
    c. Zosyn
    d. Re-exploration

    **Answer d.** (see below)

17

36. The most likely organism in the above scenario is:
    a.  Staph aureus
    b.  Clostridium perfringens
    c.  Enterococcus
    d.  E. Coli

**Answer b.** Clostridium perfringens wound infection is rare but it needs to be recognized. Patients who have a high fever immediately post-op need to have their dressing removed and their wound inspected. If wound drainage appears or there is surrounding skin changes, the patient should be immediately taken back to the OR for wide debridement. The patient is at high risk for developing necrotizing fascitis and/or myonecrosis.

Beta-hemolytic group A strep is also a potential source of early invasive wound infection early post-op.

Penicillin is the classic treatment of choice for both clostridium perfringens and beta-hemolytic group A strep, but in reality you would start a broad spectrum antibiotic until you knew what the organism was.

37. The muscles that are the 1$^{st}$ to relax with paralytics are:
    a.  Neck muscles and face
    b.  Diaphragm muscles
    c.  Extremities
    d.  Abdominal wall

**Answer a.** (see below)

38. The muscles that are last to relax with paralytics and the 1$^{st}$ to recover are the:
    a.  Neck muscles and face
    b.  Diaphragm muscles
    c.  Extremity muscles
    d.  Abdominal wall muscles

**Answer b.** The muscles of the neck and face are the 1$^{st}$ to relax with paralytics and the last to recover. The diaphragm muscles are the last to relax and the 1$^{st}$ to recover.

39. The various inhaled anesthetics have different biological characteristics. A low minimum alveolar concentration (MAC) of an inhaled anesthetic indicates:
    a. A less potent anesthetic
    b. A more lipid soluble anesthetic
    c. A very fast onset
    d. A large amount of anesthetic is required for induction

    **Answer b.** The minimum alveolar concentration of an inhaled anesthetic is the amount of anesthetic for which only 50% of patients will move with incision.

    A low minimum alveolar concentration = more lipid soluble = more potent anesthetic.

    Speed of induction is inversely proportional to solubility.

    A high alveolar concentration = less lipid soluble = less potent = faster onset.

    Nitrous oxide is the fastest working inhaled anesthetic but also has a high MAC.

40. Severe hallucinations are a common side effect of:
    a. Ketamine
    b. Etomidate
    c. Propofol
    d. Sodium thiopental

    **Answer a.** Severe hallucinations are a side effect of ketamine.

19

41. Non-depolarizing paralytics can be reversed with:
    a. Beta-blocker
    b. Alpha blocker
    c. Calcium
    d. Neostigmine

    **Answer d.** Non-depolarizing paralytics competitively block acetylcholine receptors. If you block acetylcholinesterase, you get a build up of acetylcholine which will compete against the non-depolarizing paralytic.

    Neostigmine is an inhibitor of acetylcholinesterase.

42. Of the anesthetics listed below, the one most likely to cause an allergic reaction is:
    a. Lidocaine
    b. Bupivicaine
    c. Mepivicaine
    d. Procaine

    **Answer d.** Amide type local anesthetics (all have "i" in 1ˢᵗ part of their name) such as lidocaine, bupivicaine, and mepivicaine rarely cause allergic reactions.

    Ester type anesthetics, such as procaine, cocaine, and tetracaine are more likely to cause allergic reactions because of their PABA analogue.

43. All of the following are true of local anesthetics except:
    a. These agents work by increasing the action potential threshold in peripheral nerves
    b. Work better in acidic environments
    c. Can cause seizures
    d. Ester based local anesthetics have increased allergic reactions compared to amide based

**Answer b.** Local anesthetics work by raising the action potential threshold (makes it harder to have an action potential occur so the pain sensation is not transmitted). Local anesthetics work very poorly in acidic environments (which makes it hard to anesthetize infected wounds).

44. Histamine release is characteristic of:
    a. Demerol
    b. Fentanyl
    c. Sufentanil
    d. Morphine

    **Answer d.** Morphine has a characteristic histamine release which can cause hypotension.

45. An overdose of fentanyl is treated with:
    a. Flumazenil
    b. Narcan
    c. Neostigmine
    d. Edrophonium

    **Answer b.** All narcotic agent (morphine, fentanyl, Demerol, sufentanil, etc.) overdoses can be treated with Narcan (naloxone).

46. A severe overdose of ativan is treated with:
    a. Flumazenil
    b. Narcan
    c. Neostigmine
    d. Edrophonium

    **Answer a.** Severe overdoses of benzodiazepines (ativan, valium, versed, ect.) are treated with flumazenil.

21

47. A patient undergoing a left lower lobectomy has an epidural placed containing morphine and bupivicaine. All of the following are true concerning the epidural except:

    a.   Respiratory depression is most likely due to the morphine

    b.   Hypotension and bradycardia are most like due to the bupivicaine

    c.   Epidurals are well tolerated in patients with hypertrophic cardiomyopathy

    d.   Spinal headaches can often be treated with a blood patch

**Answer c.** Hypertrophic cardiomyopathy is a contraindication to epidurals because they cause a decrease in afterload, which can be catastrophic in patients with dilated cardiomyopathy (the ventricle will collapse on itself usually at the level of the septum).

Hypotension and bradycardia which occur with epidurals are almost always related to the local anesthetic (bupivicaine) placed in the epidural.

Interestingly, although morphine can cause hypotension when given systemically, it does not occur with epidural infusion (likely because the CSF does not contain histamine releasing mast cells).

Respiratory depression is related to morphine in epidurals. Many centers place dilaudid in epidurals to avoid this side-effect.

48. Prior to performing a lung resection, the anesthesiologist attempts to intubate the patient but he is not sure if the tube is in the trachea. The best determinant of esophageal versus tracheal intubation is:

    a.   Breath sounds

    b.   Gastric sounds

    c.   Opinion of the anesthesiologist

    d.   End tidal $CO_2$

**Answer d.** The most sensitive test as to whether or not the endotracheal is placed correctly is the end tidal CO2 monitor.

49. A 65 yo man on dialysis for renal failure undergoes an elective abdominal aortic aneurysm repair. This patients ASA class is:
    a. II
    b. III
    c. IV
    d. V

**Answer c.**

Class I – healthy patient

Class II – mild disease without limitation (HTN, DM, obesity, smokers)

Class III – severe disease (stable angina, previous MI, moderate COPD)

Class IV – disease is a severe constant threat to life (unstable angina, renal or liver failure, severe COPD)

Class V – moribund patient (i.e. ruptured AAA, saddle pulmonary embolus)

Class VI – organ donor

## Fluids and Electrolytes (also see critical care section)

50. The composition of lactated ringers is:
    a. Na 154, Cl 109, K 4, Ca 2.7, HCO3 28
    b. Na 130, Cl 103, K 4, Ca 2.7, HCO3 28
    c. Na 154, Cl 109, K 4, Ca 4, HCO3 28
    d. Na 130, Cl 109, K 4, Ca 2.7, HCO3 28

    **Answer d.** Lactated Ringers is the fluid resuscitation of choice in trauma patients. Normal saline contains Na 154 mEq/L and Cl 154 mEq/L.

51. A 3 month old child has persistent vomiting associated with pyloric stenosis. The most likely metabolic change is:
    a. Hypochloremic, hypokalemic metabolic alkalosis
    b. Hyperchloremic, hypokalemic metabolic alkalosis
    c. Hypochloremic, hyperkalemic metabolic alkalosis
    d. Hyperchloremic, hyperkalemic metabolic alkalosis

    **Answer a.** A child with pyloric stenosis and vomiting is losing both water and HCl (this is the hypochloremia part and the metabolic alkalosis part of the equation).

    To compensate for the water loss, the kidney reabsorbs Na in exchange for K (this is the hypokalemia part).

    Also, the kidney recognizes that it is losing K so it exchanges K for H, which results in paradoxical aciduria.

    The end result is hypochloremic, hypokalemic, metabolic alkalosis with paradoxical aciduria.

    Treatment is volume resuscitation with K+ containing solutions (usually D10 normal saline with 10 mEq of K in children).

    In adults, this problem usually occurs with NG tube suctioning. Tx is maintenance D5 ½ NS with 20 mEq of K+.

52. What should the maintenance fluid rate be on a 50 kg boy?
    a.   120 cc/hr
    b.   90 cc/hr
    c.   60 cc/hr
    d.   30 cc/hr


**Answer b.**

For the first 10 kg, the maintenance IVF rate is 4 cc/kg/hour.
For the next 10 kg, the maintenance rate is 2 cc/kg/hour.
For anything after that, the rate is 1cc/kg/hour

For our patient, the rate should be 40 cc/hour + 20 cc/hour +
30 cc/hour = 90 cc/hr.

## Nutrition

53. A patient receives a 1000 cc bag of TPN which contains 10% dextrose and 7% protein. In addition, this patient receives 250 cc of a 20% fat emulsion solution. How many calories does this approximately represent?
    a. 1020 calories
    b. 1420 calories
    c. 1820 calories
    d. 2220 calories

    **Answer a.**
    A 1000 cc bag of 10% dextrose is equal to 100 gm of dextrose (0.10 x 1000 = 100 gm), which is 340 calories (100 gm x 3.4 calories/gm).

    A 1000 cc bag of 7% protein is equal to 70 gm of protein (0.07 x 1000 = 70 gm), which is 280 calories (70 gm x 4 calories/gm).

    A 250 cc bag of 20% fat emulsion is equivalent to 50 gm of fat (0.20 x 250 = 50), and 50 gm of fat is equivalent to 400 calories (50 gm x 8 calories/gm).

    Then just add them up 340 + 280 + 400 = 1020 calories.

54. The primary nutrition source of colonocytes is:
    a. Glutamine
    b. Short chain fatty acids
    c. Glucose
    d. Alpha-keto gluterate

    **Answer b.** (see below)

55. The primary nutrition source of small bowel is:
    a. Glutamine

b. Short chain fatty acids
c. Glucose
d. Alpha-keto gluterate

**Answer a.** (see below)

56. The primary nutrition source of cancer cells is:
    a. Glutamine
    b. Short chain fatty acids
    c. Glucose
    d. Alpha-keto gluterate

    **Answer a.** The primary source of nutrition for colonocytes is short chain fatty acids. Occasionally patients undergoing low anterior resection with a Hartman's pouch can get disuse proctitis due to lack of short chain fatty acids. The treatment of which is short chain fatty acid enemas.

    The primary source of nutrition for small bowel cells (enterocytes) is glutamine. There has been a lot of literature suggesting that glutamine enhanced tube feeds decreases gut translocation in patients with sepsis, trauma, etc. This, however, has not been definitive.

    The primary source of nutrition for neoplastic cells is glutamine.

57. During prolonged starvation, the brain switches from using glucose to using:
    a. Glutamine
    b. Short chain fatty acids
    c. Arginine
    d. Ketones

    **Answer d.** The brain switches from glucose to ketones after prolonged starvation.

27

58. Which of the following lab values is most predictive of post-operative morbidity and mortality?
    a.  Low sodium
    b.  Low potassium
    c.  Low transferrin
    d.  Low albumin

   **Answer d.** Low albumin has been directly correlated with increased morbidity and mortality following operative procedures.

59. Overfeeding patients in the intensive care unit can result in:
    a.  Prolonged intubation
    b.  Hypoglycemia
    c.  Renal failure
    d.  Hypokalemia

   **Answer a.** Overfeeding can lead to high carbohydrate build-up and increased $CO_2$ production. This makes the lungs work harder to get rid of the $CO_2$, which can tire patients out and result in prolonged ventilation.

   $CO_2$ is produced when the excess carbohydrates are converted to fat.

60. Re-feeding syndrome results in all of the following except:
    a.  Hypokalemia
    b.  Hypomagnesemia
    c.  Hyponatremia
    d.  Hypophosphatemia

   **Answer c.** Re-feeding syndrome can result in hypokalemia, hypomagnesemia, and hypophosphatemia. It occurs in patients who are severely malnourished and then start receiving appropriate nutrition. The electrolyte abnormalities can contribute to cardiac dysfunction (arrhythmias).

Re-feeding syndrome is prevented by starting nutrition at a low rate initially (10-15 kcal/kg/day).

61. Which of the following abnormalities can cause prolonged ventilation:
    a. Hypokalemia
    b. Hypomagnesemia
    c. Hyponatremia
    d. Hypophosphatemia

    **Answer d.** Hypophosphatemia can result in prolonged ventilation due to relative ATP insufficiency (need phosphate to convert ADP to ATP).

    K and Mg are important ions involved in gut motility (these should be replace in patients with a prolonged ileus).

    Deficiencies in K and Mg can also contribute to heart arrhythmias such as atrial fibrillation.

62. Respiratory quotient refers to:
    a. $CO_2$ production over $O_2$ consumption
    b. $O_2$ consumption over $CO_2$ production
    c. PEEP over FRC
    d. FRC over PEEP

    **Answer a.** The respiratory quotient refers to the amount of $CO_2$ produced in the body compared to $O_2$ consumed.

63. A respiratory quotient < 0.7 indicates:
    a. Starvation
    b. Overfeeding
    c. Pure protein nutrition
    d. Pure glucose

29

**Answer a.** (see below)

64. A respiratory quotient > 1 indicates:
    a. Starvation
    b. Overfeeding
    c. Pure protein nutrition
    d. Pure glucose

**Answer b.** Over-feeding a patient will result in the conversion of carbohydrates to fat. This conversion will cause a relative increase in $CO_2$ production compared to $O_2$ consumed. Thus, the RQ will increase.

Conversely, underfeeding a patient will result in the breakdown of fat and glycogen stores which does not increase $CO_2$. Oxygen consumption increases during starvation. In this situation, the RQ will decrease.

65. Ileal resection can result in all of the following except:
    a. Decreased $B_{12}$ and folate uptake which can result in megaloblastic anemia
    b. Decreased bile salt uptake which can cause osmotic diarrhea (bile salts) and steatorrhea ($\downarrow$ fat uptake) in colon
    c. Increased bile salt uptake which can result in the formation of gallstones
    d. Decreased oxalate binding to calcium secondary to increased intra-luminal fat. Oxalate then gets absorbed in colon, is released in urine, and can cause Ca oxalate kidney stones (hyperoxaluria)

**Answer c.** Ileal resection does <u>not</u> result in increased bile salt resorption. The rest of the answers are true.

66. The strongest layer of the bowel wall is:
    a. Mucosa
    b. Submucosa
    c. Muscularis
    d. Serosa

**Answer b.** The strongest layer of the bowel wall is the submucosa. This is where you want your sutures when doing a hand sewn bowel anastomosis.

The time point at which the small bowel is the weakest is 3-5 days.

67. All of the following are true of glycogen stores except:
    a. Glycogen is depleted 24-36 hours after starvation
    b. Glycogen is mostly stored in muscle
    c. Skeletal muscle is abundant in glucose-6-phosphatase
    d. Glycogen stays in muscle after breakdown

**Answer c.** Glycogen is mostly stored in the skeletal muscle (2/3 skeletal muscle and 1/3 liver) and is depleted 24-36 hours after starvation.

Glycogen stays in muscle after breakdown due to deficiency of glucose-6-phosphatase in muscle (glucose-6-phosphate cannot leave the cell).

## Oncology

68. Tumor cells are most sensitive to XRT during which stage of the cell cycle?
   a.  G1
   b.  S
   c.  G2
   d.  M

**Answer d.**  (see below)

69. A 60 man with unresectable lung cancer is undergoing XRT therapy.  The main target of XRT for treatment of malignancy is:
   a.  Cell wall
   b.  Proteins
   c.  RNA
   d.  DNA

**Answer d.**  Tumor cells are most sensitive to XRT during the M phase (mitosis).  This is the result of DNA damage (the main target of XRT).

70. Positron Emission Tomography scan detects:
   a.  Fluorodeoxyglucose molecules
   b.  Tumor specific proteins
   c.  Glucose 6 phosphate molecules
   d.  Glycogen molecules

**Answer a.**  PET scan detects areas that are involved in hypermetabolism.  This may include cancer, infection, or other sources of inflammation.

Specifically, the PET scanner detects the fluorodeoxyglucose molecules which are injected into the patient and accumulate in areas of high glucose metabolism.

71. PET scanning is poor at detection of metastatic disease in the:
    a. Lung
    b. Liver
    c. Adrenal gland
    d. Brain

    **Answer d.** The brain has too much metabolic activity for PET to be effective. PET, therefore, is not really useful for detecting metastases in the brain.

72. PET scanning can be difficult in which of the following sets of patients:
    a. Hypothyroidism
    b. Hyperthyroidism
    c. Diabetes
    d. Hypertension

    **Answer c.** High glucose levels (i.e. diabetics) compete with the fluorodeoxyglucose molecule used with PET. PET is therefore less effective in patients with diabetes.

73. Pulmonary fibrosis is characteristic of which of the following chemotherapy agents:
    a. Taxol
    b. Bleomycin
    c. Cisplatnin
    d. Levamisole

    **Answer b.** Bleomycin can cause pulmonary fibrosis.

74. Ototoxicity is characteristic of which of the following chemotherapy agents:
    a. Taxol

    b.   Bleomycin
    c.   Cisplatnin
    d.   Levamisole

**Answer c.** Ototoxicity is a side effect of cisplatnin.


75. Hemorrhagic cystitis is characteristic of which of the following chemotherapy agents:
    a.   Taxol
    b.   Bleomycin
    c.   Cyclophosphamide
    d.   Levamisole

**Answer c.** Hemorrhagic cystitis is a side effect of cyclophosphamide. This is prevented with the use of mesna during chemotherapy.


76. The mechanism of action for taxol is:
    a.   DNA alkylation
    b.   Inhibition of microtubule formation
    c.   Stabilization of microtubules
    d.   Inhibition of dihydrofolate reductase

**Answer c.** Taxol type drugs prevent the breakdown of microtubules. Eventually these microtubules build-up to the point at which they puncture the cell and it lyses.


77. The mechanism of action for methotrexate is:
    a.   DNA alkylation
    b.   Inhibition of microtubule formation
    c.   Stabilization of microtubules
    d.   Inhibition of dihydrofolate reductase

**Answer d.** Methotrexate causes inhibition of dihydrofolate reductase. Leucovorin rescue decreases folate (tetrahydrofolic acid) levels and reverses the effects of methotrexate.

78. Cardiotoxicity at doses greater then 500 mg/m$^2$ is characteristic of:
    a. Taxol
    b. Bleomycin
    c. Cisplatnin
    d. Adriamycin

    **Answer d.** Adriamycin is cardiotoxic at total doses of 500mg/m$^2$.

79. The mechanism of action of 5-fluorouracil is:
    a. Inhibition of thymidalate synthesis
    b. DNA alkylation
    c. Inhibition of microtubule formation
    d. Stabilization of microtubules

    **Answer a.** 5-fluorouracil inhibits thymidalate synthesis. Leucovorin increases the toxicity of 5-FU.

80. The p53 tumor suppressor gene is primarily involved in:
    a. Cell cycle regulation
    b. Cell adhesion
    c. Angiogenesis
    d. Chemotaxis

    **Answer a.** p53 is involved in cell cycle regulation and apoptosis.

81. The adenomatous polyposis coli (APC) tumor suppressor gene is primary involved in:
    a. Cell cycle regulation
    b. Cell adhesion
    c. Angiogenesis
    d. Chemotaxis

    **Answer b.** The APC gene is involved in cell adhesion and cytoskeletal function.

82. The ras proto-oncogene codes for:
    a. G protein
    b. Tyrosine kinase
    c. Platelet derived growth factor receptor
    d. Epidermal growth factor receptor

    **Answer a.** The ras proto-oncogene codes for a G protein.

83. The src proto-oncogene codes for:
    a. G protein
    b. Tyrosine kinase
    c. Platelet derived growth factor receptor
    d. Epidermal growth factor receptor

    **Answer b.** The src proto-oncogene codes for a tyrosine kinase.

84. The most common metastasis to the small bowel is:
    a. Lung cancer
    b. Colon cancer
    c. Prostate cancer
    d. Melanoma

**Answer d.** The most common metastasis to the small bowel is melanoma.

85. The genes involved in the development of colon CA include all of the following except:
    a. APC
    b. p53
    c. DCC
    d. Ret

    **Answer d.** Ret is not routinely involved in the development of colon cancer.

    The APC, p53, DCC, and k-ras genes are involved in the development of colon cancer.

86. A phase II clinical trial:
    a. Evaluates whether or not a drug is safe and at what dose
    b. Evaluates whether or not the drug is effective
    c. Evaluates whether or not the drug is better than existing therapy
    d. Involves implementation and marketing

    **Answer b.**
    Phase I trials ascertains whether or not a drug is safe and at what dose.

    Phase II trials evaluate whether or not the drug is effective.

    Phase III trials ascertains whether or not the drug is more effective than existing therapy.

    Phase IV trials deal with implementation and marketing.

87. All of the following are true of sentinel lymph node biopsy except:

37

a. Lymph nodes staining blue after lymphazurin blue dye should be resected
b. The lymph node with the highest gamma count should be resected
c. Lymph nodes within 10% of the highest gamma count should be resected
d. Patients with clinically positive nodes should definitely undergo sentinel lymph node biopsy

**Answer d.** Patients with clinically positive nodes should undergo formal lymph node dissection.

All blue nodes and nodes within 10% of the highest gamma count node should be taken.

If no dye or no gamma counts can be found in the area, formal lymph node dissection should be performed.

For a high gamma count in a lymph node basin you were not expecting (i.e. you are doing a sentinel lymph node biopsy in a patient for breast cancer and the supra-clavicular region lights up), you should sample lymph nodes in the area that has the high count if it is at least 10% of the highest count node.

In general, 1-3 lymph nodes are taken with a sentinel lymph node biopsy.

88. The most important prognostic factor for sarcomas devoid of metastases is:
    a. Node status
    b. Size of tumor
    c. Tumor grade
    d. Gender of patient

**Answer c.** The most important prognostic factor in patients with sarcoma is tumor grade.

Sarcomas rarely go to lymph nodes.

89. The most important prognostic factor for breast cancer devoid of systemic metastases is:
    a.  Node status
    b.  Size of tumor
    c.  Tumor grade
    d.  Gender of patient

    **Answer a.** The most important prognostic factor in patients with breast cancer (devoid of metastases) is nodal status (positive or negative, how many nodes, IMA vs. axillary nodes).

90. A patient has a 5 cm suspicious mass in his anterior thigh. You get an MRI and the bone, vascular structures, and nerves are not involved. You think it's a lipoma, but you are not sure. The patient should:
    a.  Have a longitudinal excisional biopsy
    b.  Have a transverse incisional biopsy
    c.  Have a transverse excisional biopsy
    d.  Have a longitudinal incisional biopsy

    **Answer d.** Patients with lesions suspicious for sarcoma should have excisional biopsy if the lesion is < 4 cm and incisional biopsy if the lesion is > 4 cm.

    Longitudinal incisions should be used so that you can easily resect the scar and close the wound after re-resection for margins (if you performed an excisional biopsy) or to remove the tumor (if you performed an incisional biopsy).

## Transplantation

91. Two weeks following kidney transplantation, a patient develops respiratory insufficiency requiring admission to the intensive care unit. Chest XR shows diffuse infiltrates and bronchial washings show cells with inclusion bodies. The most appropriate therapy is:
    a. Gangciclovir
    b. Acyclovir
    c. Bactrim
    d. Penicillin

    **Answer a.** CMV infection is common among transplant patients and forms characteristic inclusion bodies in cells (alveolar macrophages). Gangciclovir is used to treat CMV pneumonia.

92. Hyperacute rejection following organ transplantation is most often due to:
    a. ABO incompatibility
    b. Rh incompatibility
    c. Previously sensitized T cells
    d. Macrophages

    **Answer a.** Hyperacute rejection is most often due to ABO incompatibility and involves pre-formed recipient antibodies to donor antigens.

93. Hyperacute rejection is an example of hypersensitivity reaction:
    a. Type I
    b. Type II
    c. Type III
    d. Type IV

    **Answer b.** Hyperacute rejection is an example of a Type II hypersensitivity reaction.

94. Successful treatment of hyperacute rejection usually involves:
    a. Steroids
    b. Removal of the organ and re-transplantation
    c. OKT3
    d. Rapamycin

    **Answer b.** Successful treatment of hyperacute rejection usually involves removal of the organ and re-transplantation.

95. The mechanism of cyclosporin is:
    a. Binds FK binding protein
    b. Binds cyclophilin protein
    c. Inhibits purine synthesis by way of 6-mercaptopurine intermediate
    d. Binds antigens on T cells

    **Answer b.** Cyclosporin binds to the cyclophilin protein.

    This complex inhibits genes for cytokine synthesis (Il-2, IL-3, IL-4, and INF-gamma).

96. The mechanism of azathioprine is:
    a. Binds FK binding protein
    b. Binds cyclophilin protein
    c. Inhibits purine synthesis by way of 6-mercaptopurine intermediate
    d. Binds antigens on T cells

    **Answer c.** Azathioprine inhibits purine synthesis, which in effect inhibits T cells.

    The active metabolite is 6-mercaptopurine which is formed in the liver.

41

97. The monoclonal antibody that specifically blocks the CD3
molecule on T cells is:
   a. OKT3
   b. ATGAM
   c. Thymoglobulin
   d. Zenepax

**Answer a.** OKT3 binds the CD3 molecule on lymphocytes.
This inhibits formation of the T-cell receptor complex and
causes opsonization of the T-cell. This drug can be used to
treat rejection that is refractory to pulse steroids.

98. The monoclonal antibody that specifically blocks IL-2 receptors is:
   a. OKT3
   b. ATGAM
   c. Thymoglobulin
   d. Zenepax

**Answer d.** Zenepax is an antibody against human IL-2
receptors. It is often used with induction therapy immediately
after transplantation.

99. The most common malignancy following transplantation is:
   a. Lung cancer
   b. Prostate cancer
   c. Breast cancer
   d. Skin cancer

**Answer d.** The most common malignancy following
transplantation is skin cancer.

100. A positive cross-match means:
   a. There are no immunologic problems so one may proceed
      with the transplant

b.  Will likely result in only mild rejection sometime after the 1$^{st}$ week
c.  The recipient has preformed antibodies to donor antigens
d.  Both the donor and recipient are CMV positive

**Answer c.** A positive cross-match means that the recipient has preformed antibodies to donor antigens. Hyperacute rejection would likely occur if the transplant were to ensue.

101. A cross-match is performed by:
a.  Mixing donor lymphocytes with recipient serum
b.  Mixing recipient lymphocytes with donor serum
c.  Mixing donor plasma with recipient serum
d.  Mixing recipient plasma with donor serum

**Answer a.** A crossmatch is performed by mixing donor lymphocytes (which contains the antigen) with recipient serum (which contains the antibody).

102. The principal cells involved in acute rejection is:
a.  B cells
b.  T cells
c.  Macrophages
d.  Platelets

**Answer b.** The principle cells involved in acute rejection is T cells.

103. Post-transplant lymphoproliferative disorder has been most commonly linked to:
a.  HSV
b.  RSV
c.  EBV
d.  Influenza viruses

43

**Answer c.** Ebstein barr virus has been implicated in the development of post-transplant lymphoproliferative disorder.

Treatment of PTLD involves lowering immunosuppression. If the tumor fails to regress, chemo-XRT is indicated.

104. A 35 yo man POD #6 from a cadaveric renal transplantation develops a rise in creatnine. The most appropriate next step is:
    a. Emergent re-operation
    b. Angiography
    c. OKT3
    d. Ultrasound

**Answer d.** The $1^{st}$ step in the work-up of a kidney transplant recipient with an elevated creatnine or decreased urine output (or any other signs of rejection) is an ultrasound.

Ultrasound assesses vascular supply to the graft, looks for compression of the ureter, and can identify fluid collections consistent w/ either urine leaks, lymphocoeles, hematomas, or seromas. You can also perform a kidney Bx at the same time.

Some groups will empirically treat with pulse steroids while waiting for the ultrasound and biopsy results.

105. In the previous patient, the ultrasound shows flow acceleration and narrowing at the level of the arterial anastomosis. The next appropriate step is:
    a. Emergent re-operation
    b. Angiography
    c. OKT3
    d. Biopsy

**Answer b.** Angiogram with angioplasty and stent placement is the treatment of choice for a tight arterial anastomosis following kidney transplantation

106. Instead of the above, the ultrasound is normal. The most appropriate next step is:
    a. Emergent re-operation
    b. Angiography
    c. OKT3
    d. Biopsy

    **Answer d.** If there is no obvious mechanical problem with the graft, you should perform a biopsy.

107. Biopsy in the above patient shows acute tubulitis. This is consistent with:
    a. Acute rejection
    b. Urinary tract infection
    c. Chronic rejection
    d. Renal vein thrombosis

    **Answer a.** Acute tubulitis is consistent with rejection. A more severe acute rejection would involve vasculitis. This patient should be started on pulse steroids. You should follow the creatnine and likely re-biopsy the kidney after 5-7 days.

108. After being treated with pulse steroids for 1 week, you re-biopsy the patient and there is no longer any signs of rejection but there is a large fluid collection anterior the to kidney. You send the fluid off and the creatnine is 20 (serum creatnine is 0.8). The next step in management is:
    a. Explant the kidney
    b. Try to repair the cysto-ureteral anastomosis
    c. Place a stent and percutaneous drainage
    d. Nothing

45

**Answer c.** The most appropriate treatment for a urine leak (in most instances) is percutaneous drainage and placement of a ureteral stent across the anastomosis. Trying to redo the anastomosis is usually unsuccessful (although this may be appropriate if the anastomosis completely fell apart on POD #1).

109. New proteinuria in a patient following kidney transplant is most consistent with:
    a. Acute rejection
    b. Urinary tract infection
    c. Chronic rejection
    d. Renal vein thrombosis

**Answer d.** New proteinuria is most consistent with renal vein thrombosis.

110. Most common cause of acute death in a living related kidney donor is:
    a. Pulmonary embolism
    b. Hemorrhage
    c. Myocardial infarction
    d. Infection

**Answer a.** The most common cause of acute death in a living related kidney donor is pulmonary embolism.

111. Most common cause of acute death following kidney transplantation in the recipient is:
    a. Pulmonary embolism
    b. Hemorrhage
    c. Myocardial infarction
    d. Infection

**Answer c.** The most common cause of death in a kidney transplant recipient is myocardial infarction (some say stroke).

## Inflammation and cytokines

112. Thromboxane:
   a.  decreases platelet aggregation by increasing release of calcium in platelets
   b.  decreases platelet aggregation by decreasing release of calcium in platelets
   c.  increases platelet aggregation by increasing release of calcium in platelets
   d.  increases platelet aggregation by decreasing release of calcium in platelets

   **Answer c.**  Thromboxane causes platelet aggregation by increasing Ca within the platelet.  This causes exposure of the Gp IIb/IIIa receptor and platelet binding.

113. Prostacyclin:
   a.  decreases platelet aggregation and causes vasodilatation
   b.  decreases platelet aggregation and causes vasoconstriction
   c.  increases platelet aggregation and causes vasodilatation
   d.  increases platelet aggregation and causes vasoconstriction

   **Answer a.**  Prostacyclin decreases platelet aggregation and causes vasodilatation.

114. Platelet dense granules contain all of the following except:
   a.  Serotonin
   b.  Adenosine
   c.  Calcium
   d.  Platelet factor 4

   **Answer d.**  Platelet dense granules contain adenosine, serotonin, and calcium.  These granules do not contain platelet factor 4 (alpha granules have this).

115. The most potent stimulus for TNF alpha release is:
    a.  IL-1
    b.  IL-6
    c.  Lipopolysaccharide
    d.  Shock

   **Answer c.** The most potent stimulus for TNF-alpha release is lipopolysaccharide.

116. Cachexia in patients with cancer is primarily the result of:
    a.  IL-2
    b.  IL-6
    c.  IL-10
    d.  TNF-alpha

   **Answer d.** TNF-alpha promotes cachexia in patients with cancer. The mechanism is not completely understood.

## Wound healing

117. The most predominate cell type in the 1$^{st}$ 24 hours of a wound is:
    a.   PMN's
    b.   Macrophages
    c.   Lymphocytes
    d.   Fibroblasts

**Answer a.** (see below)

118. The most predominant cell type at days 3 and 4 after a wound is:
    a.   PMN's
    b.   Macrophages
    c.   Lymphocytes
    d.   Platelets

**Answer b.** (see below)

119. The most predominate cell type in a 7 day old wound is:
    a.   PMN's
    b.   Macrophages
    c.   Lymphocytes
    d.   Fibroblasts

**Answer d.**
The most predominant cell type days 0-2 is **PMN's**.
The most predominant cell type days 3-4 is **macrophages**.
The most predominant cell type from day 5 onward is **fibroblasts.**

120. The most predominant type of collagen in the body is:
    a.   Type I
    b.   Type II

50

    c.   Type III
    d.   Type IV

**Answer a.** The most predominant collagen type in the body is type I collagen.

121. The most predominant type of collagen being synthesized in a healing wound in the $1^{st}$ 24 hours is:
    a.   Type I
    b.   Type II
    c.   Type III
    d.   Type IV

**Answer c.** The most predominant collagen type being synthesized in the $1^{st}$ 48 hours of a wound is Type III collagen. This is eventually replaced with Type I collagen.

122. The maximum collagen amount in a wound occurs at:
    a.   1 week
    b.   3 weeks
    c.   8 weeks
    d.   3 months

**Answer b.** Maximum collagen accumulation occurs at 2-3 weeks. After that, the amount of collagen stays the same but continued cross-linking improves strength.

123. The most important cell involved in wound healing is:
    a.   PMN's
    b.   Macrophages
    c.   Platelets
    d.   Lymphocytes

**Answer b.** The most important cell type involved in wound healing is macrophages. Wound healing can occur without one of the other cell types except macrophages, whose cytokine and growth factor synthesis are instrumental to getting the right cells to the wound for healing to occur.

124. The most predominant collagen type in cartilage is:
   a. Type I
   b. Type II
   c. Type III
   d. Type IV

   **Answer b.** Type II cartilage is the most predominant type in cartilage.

125. Maximum tensile strength of a wound occurs at:
   a. 1 week
   b. 3 weeks
   c. 8 weeks
   d. 3 months

   **Answer c.** Maximum tensile strength occurs at 8 weeks.

126. Steroids have been show to retard wound healing. The vitamin that has been shown to prevent the negative effects of steroids on wound healing is:
   a. Vitamin A
   b. Vitamin D
   c. Vitamin E
   d. Vitamin K

   **Answer a.** Vitamin A has been shown to prevent the negative effect of steroids on wound healing.

127. Peripheral nerves regenerate at:
    a.   0.01 mm/day
    b.   0.1 mm/day
    c.   1 mm/day
    d.   5 mm/day

**Answer c.** Nerves regenerate at 1 mm/day

128. The most important factor in the healing of wounds by secondary intention is:
    a.   Tensile strength of the wound
    b.   Epithelial integrity
    c.   Platelet activating factor
    d.   Prostacyclin

**Answer b.** The most important factor in wound healing by secondary intention is epithelial integrity.

Keeping the epithelium intact over the wound avoids leakage of proteins and serum which are a set-up for infection.

Epithelial cells migrate primarily from hair follicle beds but also from the wounds edges and sweat glands.

129. The most important factor in the healing of wounds by primary intention is:
    a.   Tensile strength of the wound
    b.   Epithelial integrity
    c.   Platelet activating factor
    d.   Prostacyclin

**Answer a.** Wound healing by primary intention is dependent on the tensile strength of the wound. This is created by collagen cross-linking.

53

The sutures you place hold the wound together until appropriate collagen deposition and cross-linking can occur.

130. A patient with a large open gluteal laceration comes to clinic and to your surprise the wound is much smaller. This is primarily a result of:
   a. Lymphocytes
   b. Macrophages
   c. PMN's
   d. Myofibroblasts

   **Answer d.** Myofibroblasts participate in wound contraction. Wound contraction is better with areas of excess tissues (such as the gluteus) and poorer in areas with less excess tissue (like the lower leg).

131. All of the following are true of keloids except:
   a. They are confined to the original scar area
   b. Can be treated with silicone injections
   c. Can be treated with steroids
   d. Can be treated with XRT

   **Answer a.** Keloids are <u>not</u> confined to the original scar (hypertrophic scar tissue is). Keloids are treated with silicone injections, steroids, and XRT.

# Trauma

132. A 30 yo man involved in a motor vehicle crash suffers an isolated
     severe closed head injury. Soon after arriving at the hospital, the
     patient starts making a copious amount of urine. All of the
     following are true of this patient except:
     a. This is most consistent with diabetes insipidus
     b. The urine specific gravity in this patient is likely low
     c. Serum sodium concentration is likely high and urine
        sodium concentration is likely low
     d. This is most consistent with elevated anti-diuretic
        hormone

     **Answer d.** SIADH would result in fluid retention, not
     diuresis. Diabetes insipidus is caused by lack of ADH, which
     results in dilute urine and elevated serum Na.

133. A 25 yo man suffers a GSW to the lower abdomen. On
     exploration, the ureter above the pelvic brim is transected with a 1
     cm segment missing. The most appropriate management of this
     injury is:
     a. Re-implantation into the bladder
     b. Trans uretero-ureterostomy
     c. Re-anastomosis
     d. Percutaneous drainage

     **Answer c.** (see below)

134. A 25 yo man suffers a GSW to the lower abdomen. On
     exploration, the ureter below the pelvic brim is transected with a 1
     cm segment missing. The most appropriate management of this
     injury is:
     a. Re-implantation into the bladder
     b. Trans uretero-ureterostomy
     c. Re-anastomosis
     d. Percutaneous drainage

**Answer a.** (see below)

135. A 25 yo man suffers a GSW wound to the lower abdomen. On exploration, the ureter above the pelvic brim is transected with a 2.5 cm segment missing. The most appropriate management of this injury is:
    a.  Re-implantation into the bladder
    b.  Trans uretero-ureterostomy
    c.  Re-anastomosis
    d.  Percutaneous drainage

    **Answer d.** Full trans-section ureteral injuries can be divided into high/middle injuries (above the pelvic brim) and lower injuries (below the pelvic brim).

    Complete transections below the pelvic brim (lower injuries) are always treated with re-implantation into the bladder. This is because a cysto-ureteral anastomosis has a much higher success rate than a uretero-ureteral anastomosis (especially after trauma).

    Injuries above the pelvic brim (in the trauma setting) are handled in one of 2 ways. If there is just a short segment missing (< 2 cm), go ahead and mobilize as much ureter as you can without devascularizing it and perform re-anastomosis. Consider placing a stent in this situation.

    If more the 2 cm is missing, place a percutaneous nephrostomy tube and tie off both ends of the ureter. At a later date, a urologist can perform a uretero-ureter anastomosis or an ileal conduit.

136. A 25 yo man comes to your office 3 months after a motor vehicle accident with left chest pain. You get a CXR and see air-fluid levels in the chest. The most appropriate next step in management is:

a. Exploration through the abdomen
b. Exploration through the chest
c. Chest tube
d. Percutaneous drain

**Answer b.** The acute management of a diaphragmatic injury is to go through the abdomen. In patients with delayed presentation (> 1 week), you need to go through the chest because the patient will have adhesions which you must take down through a chest incision.

137. Diaphragm injuries:
    a. Are more common on the right
    b. Are more common on the left
    c. Occur most commonly with penetrating injury
    d. Are easy to find with CT scan

**Answer b.** Diaphragm injuries are more common with blunt trauma and are more common on the left (liver protects the right side).

Diaphragm injuries are hard to find on CT scan unless there is gross herniation.

138. A 25 yo woman involved in a motor vehicle accident resulting in a severe posterior hepatic laceration that you are trying to treat with damage control. You pack the area off and head to the ICU. She has received 20 units of blood, 10 FFP, and 10 platelets but remains hypotensive (BP 80/40). Her hematocrit is stable at 30. The most likely cause of her persistent hypotension is:
    a. Cardiac tamponade
    b. Sepsis
    c. Low calcium
    d. Low magnesium

**Answer c.** Low calcium can occur after massive transfusion. This in turn can cause hypotension.

139. A 15 yo old boy is struck in the abdomen when he goes over the handle bars on his bike. You get an abdominal CT with IV and oral contrast and you cannot identify any abnormality. The next day, you try to feed the child clears but he vomits twice. His abdomen also feels somewhat more distended compared to yesterday The most appropriate next step in management is:
    a. Repeat abdominal CT
    b. Zofran
    c. Phenergan
    d. Exploratory laparotomy

**Answer a.** (see below)

140. You repeat the child's CT scan with oral and intravenous contrast and identify a hematoma in the third portion of the duodenum. You do not see extravasation of contrast at the site. The most appropriate next step is:
    a. Exploratory laparotomy, evacuate the clot, close the duodenum
    b. Percutaneous evacuation of the clot
    c. NG tube suction and TPN
    d. Whipple

**Answer c.** The first lesson in this scenario is that if a trauma patient has a change in clinical status or is failing to progress normally (i.e., nausea and vomiting with clears), you need to repeat appropriate studies. Pancreatic injuries, small bowel tears, duodenal injuries and diaphragmatic injuries can present late.

Duodenal hematomas can occur as a delayed presentation in trauma. The 1st step is to make the diagnosis. This is probably best done with an UGI contrast study although CT scan of the abdomen with oral and IV contrast can pick these injures up.

Next you need to assess whether or not there is a contrast leak. If there is, you need to operate. If not, the management is NPO and TPN for up to 3 weeks. The vast majority of these resolve with conservative management.

141. A 22 yo man suffers a severe pelvis fracture and has hematuria. You get a retrograde cystourethrogram and see an extraperitoneal bladder rupture. The most appropriate therapy for this patient is:
    a. Foley drainage for 7 days
    b. Exploratory laparotomy
    c. Nothing
    d. Cystectomy

    **Answer a.** The most appropriate therapy for an extra-peritoneal bladder rupture is urinary catheter drainage for 7 days.

    The most appropriate therapy for an intra-peritoneal bladder rupture is laparotomy and surgical repair.

142. A 25 yo man suffers a posterior knee dislocation with loss of pulse. You are able to get the knee back in place and a pulse is now present. The most appropriate next step in this patient's management is:
    a. Nothing else
    b. Heparin
    c. Exploration
    d. Angiogram

    **Answer d.** Posterior knee dislocations have a high incidence of popliteal artery injury. Angiogram is mandatory.

143. A 20 yo man suffers a gunshot wound to the right chest. You place a chest tube in the emergency room and get back 2000 cc. The most appropriate step in this patients management is:
   a.   Chest CT
   b.   CXR
   c.   Clamp the chest tube
   d.   Go to OR for a right thoracotomy

**Answer d.** Criteria for going to the OR with chest tube placement in trauma are:
> 1500 cc with initial placement
> 250 cc/hr for the 1$^{st}$ 3 hours
2500 for the 1$^{st}$ 24 hours
bleeding with instability

A left thoracotomy would be indicated in this patient (instead of a right thoracotomy) if the patient did not have a pulse, at which time you would open the pericardium and clamp the aorta.

144. All of the following are true of tracheobronchial injuries except:
   a.   They are more common on the right
   b.   Breathing may be worsened after insertion of chest tube
   c.   Is one of the very few conditions in which clamping the chest tube may be beneficial
   d.   Approach to the proximal left mainstem (< 1 cm from the carina) is best carried out through a left thoracotomy

**Answer d.** Tracheo-bronchial injuries are more common on the right because the take-off of the RUL occurs at shorter distance from the carina compare to the LUL. This creates a less flexible segment which is more prone to tearing.

Breathing can be severely compromised after placing a chest tube to suction on the affected side. Essentially, the patient can take a deep breath in but it goes right out the chest tube (air leak bubbling will get more severe in the water seal chamber). This is one of the few indications in which clamping the chest tube may help breathing (you rarely ever want to clamp a chest tube in trauma because of the risk of tension pneumothorax).

The approach to right sided injuries, injuries to the trachea itself, and injures to the proximal 1cm of the left mainstem is through a right thoracotomy. The aorta is in the way for repair of proximal left mainstem injuries and injuries of the trachea if you try to go from the left.


145. A 26 yo woman is involved in a severe MVA. She is hypotensive (BP 80/40, HR 120), intubated, and has a distended abdomen. She also has a pelvic fracture. You give her 2 liters of lactated ringers and then start transfusing blood however she remains hypotensive. The most appropriate next step in management is:
    a. Abdomen and Pelvic CT
    b. Angiogram
    c. Diagnostic peritoneal lavage or FAST scan
    d. Exploratory laparotomy


**Answer c.** This is a very frequent occurrence in busy trauma centers. Put simply, in a hypotensive patient, you need to figure out if the bleeding is from the:
    abdomen
    pelvis
    chest
    extremities

The 1st test in this patient should be a DPL or FAST scan.

If this is positive, go to the OR.

If this is negative (and you are reasonably sure the source of the bleed is not the chest - which is usually assessed by physical exam and CXR) fix the pelvis in the ER if orthopaedics is standing there and waiting, but otherwise go to angiography as quickly as possible for embolization.

Wrapping a sheet around the pelvis is a method used by many centers to temporarily tamponade the bleeding while setting up for angiography.

146. The fast scan is negative in the above patient. The most appropriate next step in management is:
    a.  Abdominal and Pelvic CT
    b.  Angiogram
    c.  OR for external fixator to pelvic fracture
    d.  Exploratory laparotomy

**Answer b.** The next appropriate move is to go to angiogram for embolization of appropriate pelvic vessels.

You would not want to go to the OR for pelvic fixation in this situation (although using the sheet method of bringing the displaced pelvis together on your way to angio is acceptable).

147. A 29 yo man is shot in the abdomen and you explore him. He has a severe anterior liver injury that you are trying to treat but blood keeps welling up out of the liver bed and you are not able to control it. You decide to perform a Pringle maneuver which is:
    a.  Clamping of the portal triad
    b.  Clamping the IVC
    c.  Placing an atrio-caval shunt
    d.  Packing off the area and heading to the ICU

**Answer a.** The Pringle maneuver involves clamping the portal triad which is located in the hepato-duodenal ligament. Serial clamping for 15 minutes and off for five minutes is a reasonable method of performing the Pringle maneuver.

148. The Pringle maneuver fails to control bleeding from:
    a.  Right hepatic artery
    b.  Left hepatic artery
    c.  Portal vein
    d.  Hepatic veins

**Answer d.** The Pringle maneuver will not control bleeding from the hepatic veins (connected to the IVC posteriorly).

149. All of the following are indications for angiogram of an extremity except:
    a.  Injury to anatomically related nerve
    b.  History of severe blood loss from the injury
    c.  Large hematoma
    d.  Active hemorrhage

**Answer d.** Active hemorrhage is an indication to go to the OR, not get an angiogram.

Major (hard) signs of vascular injury:

    Active hemorrhage is present
    Pulse deficit
    Expanding or pulsatile hematoma
    Distal ischemia
    Bruit or thrill is present

    Tx: For any of the above, go emergently to OR for exploration

Moderate (soft) signs of vascular injury:

    History of hemorrhage at the scene
    Anatomically related nerve deficit
    A large stable hematoma
    Injury close to major artery (i.e. GSW to the medial thigh)
    ABI < 0.9
    Unequal pulses

    Dx: For any of the above, go to angiography

150. You perform a DPL on a patient involved in a motor vehicle accident which is positive. The patient has remained hypotensive despite blood resuscitation. The patient has a blown pupil on the right. The most appropriate next step in management is:
    a. Head CT
    b. Abdominal CT
    c. Head and abdominal CT
    d. Go to OR

**Answer d.** A positive DPL in a hypotensive patient means you go to the OR for laparotomy. In the ABC's scheme you need to take care of C (circulation) before assessing the head injury.

151. While in the OR, this patient should undergo:
    a. Laparotomy only
    b. Laparotomy followed by head CT
    c. Laparotomy and Burr hole placement
    d. Burr hole placement only

**Answer c.** While in the OR, you should place a Burr hole to decompress the side with the blown pupil. This is placed 5 cm anterior and 5 superior to the external auditory canal (frontal bone).

Another option could be to just place an ICP bolt and check the pressure, with placement of a Burr hole if the pressure is elevated (although just doing the Burr hole is probably the best treatment).

152. A 22 yo man suffers a GSW to the left flank and the patient is hypotensive but has a pulse. You start bolusing the patient with 2 liters of fluid. The most appropriate next step is:
    a. Angiography
    b. CT scan
    c. Left thoracotomy
    d. Laparotomy

**Answer d.** Laparotomy. This patient is hypotensive with a GSW to the abdomen. The only place you should be is in the OR.

153. You perform your laparotomy in the above patient, pack everything off, and notice a large, left sided retroperitoneal hematoma that extends above the level of the celiac artery. The patient is still hypotensive (BP 70/40) now after 6 units of blood. The most appropriate next step is:
    a. Mattox maneuver
    b. Cattel maneuver
    c. Pelvic embolization
    d. Infra-diaphragmatic control of the aorta

    **Answer d.** Because the hematoma extends above the celiac artery, a Mattox maneuver is not going to give you the proper exposure.

    The moves in this scenario are to either perform a left thoracotomy and clamp the aorta or place an infra-diaphragmatic clamp across the aorta until you get control of the situation.

154. You clamp the infra-diaphragmatic aorta in the above patient, perform a Mattox maneuver, and find the left renal vein is completely avulsed from the IVC. The most appropriate next step is:
    a. Replace infra-diaphragmatic clamp w/ a supra-renal clamp, oversew renal vein and ligate IVC connection
    b. Replace infra-diaphragmatic clamp with supra-renal clamp, perform primary repair
    c. Left nephrectomy
    d. Pack and go to the ICU

**Answer a.** The left renal vein has adrenal vein and gonadal vein collaterals making ligation of the left renal vein safe.

The right renal vein does <u>not</u> have these collaterals and you would have to either perform a re-anastomosis on that side or perform a nephrectomy if the patient was persistently hypotensive and you didn't have the time to perform an anastomosis.

155. A 22 yo man suffers a GSW to the right flank. During laparotomy, you notice bile stained fluid in the right upper quadrant. The most appropriate next step is:
    a.   Endoscopy
    b.   Gastrostomy
    c.   Whipple
    d.   Kocher maneuver

**Answer d.** The most appropriate move in this situation is to perform a Kocher maneuver which entails mobilizing the duodenum and examining the duodenum, the portal triad, and the head of the pancreas.

156. You start to perform your Kocher maneuver in the above patient and find that the 1$^{st}$ and proximal 2$^{nd}$ portions of the duodenum are completely blown out proximal to the common bile duct. The most appropriate next step is:
    a.   Whipple
    b.   Oversew proximal and distal portions of the duodenum, then gastro-jejunostomy
    c.   Proximal duodeno-jejunostomy and distal duodeno-jejunostomy
    d.   Place drains

**Answer b.** For an injury that is proximal to the ampulla of vater, you can staple off the proximal and distal ends of the duodenal injury and perform a gastro-jejunostomy. You can do this because the ampulla of Vater is not involved in the injury and will still drain distally. Food, however, will now go through the gastro-jejunostomy.

Remember to place drains.

If the injury involves the duodenum distal to the ampulla of vater, you will need a duodeno-jejunostomy to control biliary flow.

If the ampulla itself is destroyed (functional whipple), you can lay drains initially if the patient is unstable (most surgeons would just place drains initially) but at some point the patient will need a formal whipple.

157. A 25 yo man involved in a motor vehicle accident will open his eyes only to painful stimuli, does not form words but mumbles, and withdraws to pain. This patient's Glasgow Coma Score is:
    a.  10
    b.  8
    c.  6
    d.  4

**Answer b.** Open eyes to painful stimuli is 2, incomprehensible sounds is 2, and withdrawals from pain is 4. $2 + 2 + 4 = 8$

**Glasgow Coma Scale (GCS)**

**Motor Function**

> **6** follows commands
> **5** localizes to the pain site
> **4** withdrawals from the pain
> **3** flexion with painful stimuli (decorticate)
> **2** extension with painful stimuli (decerebrate)
> **1** no response to painful stimuli

**Verbal Response**

> **5** oriented x 3

4 confused but responds
3 inappropriate words with speech
2 incomprehensible sounds (grunting)
1 no response verbally

**Eye opening**

4 spontaneous eye opening
3 opens eyes to command
2 opens eyes to pain
1 no response to eye opening

158. The above patient is having difficulty maintaining his airway so you intubate him. Head CT shows loss of sulci and compression of cisterns so you place an intra-cerebral monitoring catheter. All of the following are true of cerebral perfusion pressure except:
    a. In general, a cerebral perfusion pressure of 70 is sufficient
    b. Cerebral perfusion pressure = mean arterial pressure – intracranial pressure
    c. Mannitol can help lower intra-cranial pressure
    d. Hypoventilation benefits these patients

    **Answer d.** In general, a cerebral perfusion pressure > 60 is sufficient.

    Mannitol helps increase cerebral perfusion pressure by drawing water out of the brain (which decreases ICP).

    Mild hyperventilation (pCO2 30-35) helps these patients by causing mild cerebral vasoconstriction which limits brain edema.

159. A 27 yo man is in the ICU 6 hours after splenectomy following a motor vehicle accident. The patient had a prolonged transport time and received 20 units of blood prior to arrival. Currently, his peak airway pressures are 65 (plateaus 50), his abdomen is distended, he is not making any urine, and his bladder pressure is 40. His CVP is 18. The most appropriate maneuver in this patient is:

a. Increase PEEP
b. Volume resuscitation
c. Decompressive laparotomy
d. CT scan

**Answer c.** This patient has classic signs of abdominal compartment syndrome. Objectively, a bladder pressure > 25-30 suggests abdominal compartment syndrome. Decreased urine output (from compression of the IVC resulting in decreased cardiac output) and elevated ventilation pressures are part of the syndrome.

Treatment of abdominal compartment syndrome is decompressive laparotomy.

## Critical Care

160. The most common cause of post-operative renal failure in a patient with normal pre-operative renal function is:
   a.  Sepsis
   b.  Hypotension intra-op
   c.  Drug toxicity
   d.  Operative injury to the renal system

   **Answer b.** The most common cause of acute renal failure post-op is hypotension intra-op.

161. All of the following are most often associated with a decrease in SVO2 (mixed venous oxygen saturation) except:
   a.  Myocardial infarction
   b.  Cardiac tamponade
   c.  Hemorrhagic shock
   d.  Septic shock

   **Answer d.** A decrease in SVO2 is caused by either decreased delivery of oxygen to the periphery or increased consumption.

   Delivery problems can be the result of a low cardiac output, decreased oxygen carrying capacity (low Hct), or a low oxygen saturation.

   Increased oxygen consumption can occur with malignant hyperthermia.

   Septic shock usually results in an increase in SVO2 due to shunting.

162. All of the following are associated with an increase in SVO2 except:
   a.  Septic shock
   b.  Left to right cardiac shunt (atrial level)

c.  Cirrhosis
d.  Cardiogenic shock


**Answer d.** An increase in SVO2 can occur with anything that causes a left to right shunt or that causes a decreased oxygen consumption in the periphery.

A left to right cardiac (at the atrial level) defect, cirrhosis, and septic shock all result in shunting.

Cyanide toxicity would result in decreased oxygen consumption and an elevated SVO2.

Cardiogenic shock would result in a lower SVO2


163. All of the following shift the oxygen dissociation curve to the left except:
    a.  Decreased CO2
    b.  Low temperature
    c.  High pH
    d.  2-3 DPG


**Answer d.** Items that cause a left shift (oxygen becomes more bound to hemoglobin) include decreased CO2, decreased temp, and high pH.

Items that cause a right shift include low pH, increased CO2, 2-3 DPG, and ATP.


164. You place a swan ganz catheter in a 70 kg adult male through the left subclavian vein and get a wedge pressure. The approximate distance into the patient should be:
    a.  45 cm
    b.  50 cm
    c.  55 cm
    d.  60 cm


71

**Answer c.** The approximate swan distances to wedge are:
Right subclavian – 45 cm
Right IJ – 50 cm
Left subclavian – 55 cm
Left IJ – 60 cm

If you place a swan-ganz catheter and wedge it but the distance is significantly longer than expected (8 cm or greater), you likely have a loop or your catheter is in the wrong place.

165. The mechanism of activated protein C in the treatment of patients with multi-system organ failure and sepsis is:
    a.   Activation of the clotting cascade
    b.   Platelet inhibition
    c.   Platelet activation
    d.   Fibrinolysis

**Answer d.** Activated protein C helps in the treatment of sepsis by increasing fibrinolysis.

166. Which sample of blood will have the lowest oxygen tension?
    a.   Coronary sinus
    b.   Femoral vein
    c.   Portal vein
    d.   Renal vein

**Answer a.** The coronary sinus has the lowest oxygen tension. The heart consumes a lot of oxygen and a typical saturation in the coronary sinus is 30%.

167. Which sample of blood will have the highest oxygen tension?
    a.   Coronary sinus
    b.   Femoral vein

c.  Portal vein
d.  Renal vein

**Answer d.** The kidney receives 25% of the cardiac output for the purpose of clearing solutes and regulating water in the body. This process does not require a large amount of oxygen expenditure. The renal vein therefore has a relatively high oxygen saturation (80%).

168. A 55 yo man goes into cardiac shock after a CABG operation despite aggressive inotropic support. You place an intra-aortic balloon and get a CXR. The balloon tip level should be:
    a.  1 cm above the iliac artery
    b.  1 cm above the renal artery
    c.  2 cm above the celiac artery
    d.  2 cm below the top of the aortic arch

**Answer d.** The tip of an aortic balloon pump should be 2 cm below the top of the aortic arch. Any higher than that, you run the risk of occluding the arch vessels. Any lower than that and you run the risk of occluding the mesenteric arteries.

169. IABP improvement in coronary flow is primarily due to:
    a.  Afterload reduction
    b.  Resting the heart
    c.  Diastolic augmentation
    d.  Decreased heart rate

**Answer c.** Coronary perfusion to the heart occurs primarily during diastole. During diastole, the IABP inflates and improves perfusion to the coronaries.

170. Proper triggering of IABP should be:
    a.  Inflation with T wave and deflation on P wave

73

b. Inflation on P wave and deflation on T wave
c. Rapid inflation and deflation after the P wave
d. Rapid inflation and deflation after the T wave

**Answer a.** The intra-aortic balloon pump should deflate on the p wave and inflate on the T wave. The IABP is deflated during systole and inflated during diastole.

171. Each of the following drugs causes stimulation of adenylate cyclase except:
   a. Dopamine
   b. Dobutamine
   c. Epinephrine
   d. Milrinone

**Answer d.** Milrinone works by inhibiting cAMP phosphodiesterase (which increases cAMP).

172. Treatment for nipride toxicity is:
   a. Amyl nitrate, then sodium nitrite
   b. Methylene blue
   c. Oxygen
   d. Vitamin C

**Answer a.** The treatment for nipride toxicity (cyanide toxicity) is amyl nitrite, followed by sodium nitrite.

173. Treatment for methemoglobinemia is:
   a. Amyl nitrate, then sodium nitrite
   b. Methylene blue
   c. Oxygen
   d. Vitamin C

**Answer b.** The treatment for methemoglobinemia is methylene blue.

174. Treatment for carbon monoxide poisoning is primarily:
    a. Amyl nitrate, then sodium nitrite
    b. Methylene blue
    c. Oxygen
    d. Vitamin C

**Answer c.** The treatment of choice for carbon monoxide poisoning is oxygen. For severe poisoning, hyperbaric oxygen therapy can be used.

175. While trying to treat a patient with severe ARDS, you start to increase the PEEP to improve oxygenation. After doing this, you notice a decrease in urine output. The mechanism of decreased urine output with increased PEEP is:
    a. Compartment syndrome
    b. Decreased cardiac output
    c. Reduced oxygenation
    d. Retained $CO_2$

**Answer b.** Progressively increasing PEEP will eventually decrease cardiac output as a result of decreased preload. Adding PEEP prevents blood from tranversing the pulmonary capillaries, resulting in decreased pre-load.

176. In the above patient, PEEP improves oxygenation by:
    a. Increasing functional residual capacity
    b. Increasing tidal volumes
    c. Increasing respiratory rate
    d. Increasing residual volume

75

**Answer a.** Positive end expiratory pressure improves oxygenation by improving the functional residual capacity (FRC). This effectively keeps the alveoli open at the end of the breath so that oxygen exchange can continue.

177. All of the following are true of lung dead space except:
   a. Refers mostly to the conductance portion of the airway
   b. Is about 150 ml in most adults
   c. Refers to areas that are ventilated and not perfused
   d. Refers to areas that are perfused but not ventilated

**Answer c.** Dead space is the area of lung that is ventilated but not perfused. In normal individuals, this is about 150 cc and refers mostly to the conduction portion of the airways (everything proximal to the respiratory bronchioles).

Pathology which can increase dead space includes excessive PEEP (collapses the alveolar capillaries), PE, ARDS, and pulmonary hypertension.

Increased dead space can lead to $CO_2$ build-up.

178. Vital capacity refers to:
   a. Volume of air in lung after maximal exhalation
   b. Volume of air left in lung after normal exhalation
   c. Maximal amount of air exhaled after maximal inhalation
   d. Volume of air with normal inspiration and exhalation

**Answer c.** Vital capacity is the maximal amount of air exhaled after a maximal inhalation.

179. Residual volume refers to:
   a. Volume of air in the lung after maximal exhalation
   b. Volume of air left in lung after normal exhalation
   c. Maximal amount of air exhaled after maximal inhalation

d.    Volume of air with normal inspiration and exhalation

**Answer a.**  Residual volume is the volume of air left in the lung after maximal exhalation.  This represents about 20% of total lung volume.

180. Tidal volume refers to:
    a.    Volume of air in lung after maximal exhalation
    b.    Volume of air left in lung after normal exhalation
    c.    Maximal amount of air exhaled after maximal inhalation
    d.    Volume of air exhaled with normal inspiration and exhalation

**Answer d.**  Tidal volume is the volume of air exhaled with normal inspiration and exhalation.

181. Functional residual capacity refers to:
    a.    Volume of air in lung after maximal exhalation
    b.    Volume of air left in lung after normal exhalation
    c.    Maximal amount of air exhaled after maximal inhalation
    d.    Volume of air with normal inspiration and exhalation

**Answer b.**  Functional residual capacity is the volume of air left in the lung after a normal exhalation (FRC = residual volume + expiratory reserve volume).

182. Post-op day 1 after a right upper lobectomy, your patient has a fever to 102.0.  The most likely source of the fever is:
    a.    PMN's
    b.    Platelets
    c.    Macrophages
    d.    Lymphocytes

**Answer c.** Alveolar macrophages are activated with atelectasis and cause fever.

183. The cytokine which induces the fever in the above patient is:
    a. IL-1
    b. IL-6
    c. IL-8
    d. IL-10

**Answer a.** IL-1 is released by macrophages and acts on the hypothalamus to cause fever.

184. The specific action of the enzyme renin is:
    a. Converts angiotensinogen to angiotensin I
    b. Converts angiotensin I to angiotensin II
    c. Causes release of aldosterone
    d. Cause absorption of Na

**Answer a.** Renin is released from the kidney and converts angiotensinogen to angiotensin I.

Renin is released in response to decreased pressure at the juxta-glomerular apparatus and to increased Na concentration sensed by the macula densa.

185. The specific action of angiotensin converting enzyme is:
    a. Converts angiotensinogen to angiotensin I
    b. Converts angiotensin I to angiotensin II
    c. Causes release of aldosterone
    d. Cause absorption of Na

**Answer b.** Angiotensin converting enzyme converts angiotensin I to angiotensin II.

Angiotensin II primarily causes the release of aldosterone.

Angiotensin II also causes vasoconstriction, increased heart rate and increased contractility.

Angiotensin converting enzyme inhibitors (ACE inhibitors) prevent the formation of angiotensin II.

186. The highest concentration of angiotensin converting enzyme is in:
    a.  liver
    b.  kidney
    c.  lung
    d.  bone

**Answer c.** The highest concentration of angiotensin converting enzyme is in the lung.

187. All of the following are true of aldosterone except:
    a.  Causes reabsorption of Na
    b.  Causes excretion of H and K ions
    c.  Acts at the distal convoluted tubule
    d.  Primarily acts on protein kinase C

**Answer d.** Aldosterone causes the resorption of Na and excretion of H and K at the distal convoluted tubule by stimulating the transcription of Na/K ATPase and Na/H ATPase. This effectively causes more water reabsorption.

188. A patient stops making urine after surgery. All of the following values are consistent with pre-renal renal failure except:
    a.  Urine Na 5
    b.  BUN/Cr ratio 35
    c.  FeNa = 0.1%
    d.  Urine osmolality 200 mOsm

**Answer d.** All of the following are consistent with pre-renal azotemia:
FeNa < 1%
Urine Na < 20
BUN/Cr ratio > 20
Urine osmolality > 500 mOsm

189. Which of the following is the most sensitive test for diagnosing pre-renal versus intrinsic renal failure:
   a. Urine sodium
   b. Urine creatnine
   c. FeNa
   d. Urine potassium

**Answer c.** FeNa is the most sensitive test for diagnosing what type of renal failure is occurring.

190. FeNa is:
   a. [ (Urine creatnine/Plasma creatnine) / (Urine sodium/Plasma sodium)]
   b. [(Urine sodium/Plasma sodium) / (Urine creatnine/Plasma creatnine)]
   c. [(Plasma sodium/Urine sodium) / (Urine creatnine/Plasma creatnine)]
   d. [(Urine sodium/Plasma sodium) / (Plasma creatnine/Urine creatnine)]

**Answer b.** This is the formula for FeNa.

191. Which of the following extubation criteria parameters is most sensitive for predicting successful extubation:
   a. Minute ventilation
   b. Rapid shallow breathing index (respiratory rate/tidal volume)

c. PO2 of 60 mmHg
d. PCO2 of 45 mmHg

**Answer b.** Several studies have now shown that the rapid shallow breathing index is the most sensitive parameter for predicting successful extubation (although nothing is 100%).

192.All of the following are complications of ketorolac (Toradol) except:
    a. Bleeding
    b. Renal failure
    c. Ulcers
    d. Peripheral neuropathy

**Answer d.** Side effects of toradol include bleeding, potential for renal failure (should be used with caution in patients > 65 or elevated Cr), and ulcers.

Peripheral neuropathy is a potential side effect of metronidazole.

193.The most sensitive test for adrenal insufficiency is:
    a. Corticotrophin stimulation test
    b. 24 urine cortisol
    c. Random serum cortisol
    d. Serum ACTH level

**Answer a.** The most sensitive test for adrenal insufficiency is the corticotrophin stimulation test.

194.A ventilated patient has the following arterial blood gas values: pH 7.50, CO2 55, HCO3 35. This condition is most likely caused by:
    a. Poor minute ventilation
    b. Aggressive NG tube suctioning

81

    c. Renal failure
    d. Severe sepsis

**Answer b.** The ABG presented suggests a metabolic alkalosis. Of the items listed, NGT suctioning is most likely to cause a metabolic alkalosis.

195. A ventilated patient has the following arterial blood gas values: pH 7.50, CO 24, HCO3 18. This condition is most likely caused by:
    a. Low minute ventilation
    b. NGT suctioning
    c. Renal failure
    d. High minute ventilation

**Answer d.** The ABG presented suggests a respiratory alkalosis. Of the items presented, high minute ventilation is most likely to cause a respiratory alkalosis. You can correct this by either decreasing respiratory rate or decreasing tidal volumes.

196. A ventilated patient has the following arterial blood gas values: pH 7.25, CO2 70, HCO3 35. This condition is most likely caused by:
    a. Poor minute ventilation
    b. NGT suctioning
    c. Renal failure
    d. Severe sepsis

**Answer a.** The ABG presented is most consistent with a respiratory acidosis. Of the items listed, poor minute ventilation is most likely to give you a respiratory acidosis. You can correct this by either increasing respiratory rate or tidal volumes.

197. A ventilated patient has the following arterial blood gas values: pH 7.26, CO 28, HCO3 18. This condition is most likely caused by:
    a. Poor minute ventilation
    b. NGT suctioning
    c. Renal failure
    d. High minute ventilation

**Answer c.** The ABG presented is most consistent with metabolic acidosis. Of the items listed, renal failure is most likely to give you a metabolic acidosis.

198. All of the following concerning pulmonary artery catheters are true except:
    a. Excessive PEEP can artificially increase wedge pressure
    b. Excessive PEEP can artificially decrease wedge pressure
    c. Zone III of the lung is the optimal site of placement
    d. The balloon should be inflated when advancing the catheter

**Answer b.** Excessive PEEP can artificially increase wedge pressures.

The optimal site of placement of the PA catheter is in zone III (bases usually) of the lung to avoid the effects of pulmonary pressures on wedge pressures.

The balloon on the swan should be inflated when advancing it and deflated when pulling it back.

199. A critical care patient has the following pulmonary artery catheter values: cardiac index 1.8, systemic vascular resistance 3000, and wedge pressure of 5. This is most consistent with:
    a. Septic shock
    b. Hypovolemic shock
    c. Cardiogenic shock
    d. Neurogenic shock

**Answer b.** Poor cardiac index, poor filling pressures and a high SVR suggests hypovolemic shock.

200. A critical care patient has the following pulmonary artery catheter values: cardiac index 5.0, systemic vascular resistance 500, and wedge pressure of 7. This is most consistent with:
    a. Septic shock
    b. Hypovolemic shock
    c. Cardiogenic shock
    d. Neurogenic shock

    **Answer a.** An elevated cardiac index of 5, a low SVR of 500, and a wedge pressure of 7 suggests septic shock.

201. A critical care patient has the following pulmonary artery catheter values: cardiac index 1.8, systemic vascular resistance 3000, and wedge pressure of 28. This is most consistent with:
    a. Septic shock
    b. Hypovolemic shock
    c. Cardiogenic shock
    d. Neurogenic shock

    **Answer c.** A cardiac index of 1.8, SVR of 3000 and wedge pressure of 28 is most consistent with cardiogenic shock.

202. A critical care patient has the following pulmonary artery catheter values: cardiac index 2.0, systemic vascular resistance 500, and wedge pressure of 5. This is most consistent with:
    a. Septic shock (early)
    b. Hypovolemic shock
    c. Cardiogenic shock
    d. Neurogenic shock

**Answer d.** A cardiac index of 2.0, SVR of 500, and wedge pressure of 5 is most consistent with neurogenic shock.

(note that late, end stage septic shock could present like this as the heart starts to give out but the answer above states early septic shock)

203. A patient with ARDS following an inhalation injury has an oxygenation saturation of 90% on 90% FiO2 with an SVO2 of 55. The patient's ABG is pH 7.35, pO2 of 60, and pCO2 60. The patient has a cardiac output of 5, and a hemoglobin of 8. Oxygen delivery will increase the most by:
    a.   Increasing cardiac output by 1
    b.   Increasing hemoglobin by 2
    c.   Increasing FIO2 by 10%
    d.   Decreasing CO2 by 10%

**Answer b:**

The formula for oxygen delivery is:
CO x [(Hgb x 1.34 x O2 saturation) + (0.003 x pO2)]

Decreasing the CO2 will <u>not</u> have any effect on the equation

Increasing FiO2 from 90% to 100% will likely not have much effect (with severe ARDS, increasing the FiO2 from 90% to 100% will not really affect oxygenation).

That leaves cardiac output and hematocrit.

Increasing the cardiac output by 1 results in:
   6 x [(8 x 1.34 x .90) + (0.003 x 60) = 57.9

Increasing the hemoglobin by 2 results in:
   5 x [(10 x 1.34 x .90) + (0.003 x 60) = 60.3

Thus, increasing the hemoglobin by 2 will have more effect than increasing the cardiac output by 1.

204. All of the following are true of nitric oxide except:
    a.  Increases cAMP
    b.  The precursor is arginine
    c.  It is primarily released from vascular endothelium
    d.  The receptor is guanylate cyclase

**Answer a.** Arginine is the precursor to nitric oxide. NO acts on guanylate cyclase to increase cGMP and cause vasodilatation.

205. All of the following are true of atrial natriuretic peptide except:
    a.  Released from the atria when stretched
    b.  Causes natriuresis and diuresis
    c.  Is an inherent method of removing excess volume in patients with congestive heart failure
    d.  Is a steroid hormone

**Answer d.** Atrial natriuretic peptide is released when the atrium are stretched (which occurs with volume overload). The peptide inhibits Na absorption and water absorption at the collecting ducts.

206. The ventilation strategy that has been most effective in patients with ARDS in terms of morbidity and mortality is:
    a.  volume control ventilation
    b.  pressure control ventilation
    c.  permissive hypoxia
    d.  Strict control of CO2 in normal ranges

**Answer b.** Pressure control ventilation to avoid barotrauma and permissive hypercapnea (allowing an elevated CO2) while correcting the pH with HCO3- has been the most effective mode of ventilation in patients with ARDS. Other maneuvers, such as prone and supine positioning can also be used.

207. The initial treatment of choice in a patient with hyperkalemia and
arrhythmias is:
  a.  Insulin and glucose
  b.  Calcium gluconate
  c.  Kaexylate
  d.  Dialysis

**Answer b.** Although all of these agents are used in patients
with hyperkalemia, a patient that is having arrhythmias as a
result of the hyperkalemia should receive Ca-gluconate $1^{st}$ to
stabilize cardiac muscle cell membranes.

**Burns**

208. A 28 yo man suffers severe $2^{nd}$ and $3^{rd}$ degree burns over 60% of total body surface area after falling asleep in bed with a cigarette. He is intubated and currently undergoing appropriate fluid resuscitation. The patient has $3^{rd}$ degree burns across his entire chest extending to his back. The patient also has a circumferential burn to his right arm with decreased perfusion to his right hand. The next appropriate step in management is:
    a. Escharotomy
    b. Arm elevation
    c. Thrombectomy of the right brachial artery
    d. TPA

**Answer a.** Patients with circumferential $2^{nd}$ and $3^{rd}$ degree burns and poor distal perfusion should undergo escharotomy to that extremity.

209. Despite escharotomy in the above patient, he still has decreased perfusion in his right arm. The most appropriate next step is:
    a. Arm elevation
    b. Thrombectomy of the right brachial artery
    c. TPA
    d. Fasciotomy

**Answer d.** Occasionally for deep burns, escharotomy is not enough and fasciotomy is required. For the arm, opening the dorsal and ventral compartments is required.

210. After appropriate treatment of the above patient's arm, you notice that his tidal volumes on the ventilator are falling and the patient is developing high mean and peak airway pressures (50 and 65 cm H20, respectively). You paralyze him and place him on pressure control ventilation but his CO2 rises to 75 mmHg and you still have elevated airway pressures. His tidal volumes are only 300 cc. The most appropriate next step is:

88

    a.   Aggressive diuresis
    b.   Inhaled NO
    c.   High frequency ventilation
    d.   Escharotomy

**Answer d.** Patients with severe burns across the chest can have trouble with ventilation due to decreased chest wall compliance (from both the burn and from edema with subsequent fluid resuscitation).

211. Approximately 12 hours later, the previous patient has improved ventilation after appropriate therapy but now stops making urine despite following the Parkland Formula protocol. The next appropriate step is:
    a.   Double to fluid resuscitation
    b.   Lasix
    c.   Dobutamine drip
    d.   Place a central line

**Answer d.** Hard to know right away the cause of the patient's renal failure.

Could be due to hypovolemia (the Parkland formula can underestimate fluid requirement with ETOH, inhalational injury, electrical injury, or in post-escharotomy patients).

This could also be due to acute tubular necrosis from myoglobinuria.

It is best not to guess in this patient. Place a central line, shoot some numbers, and figure it out.

212. You place a central line in the above patient and his CVP is 18. The most likely cause of his renal failure is:
    a.   Cardiogenic shock
    b.   Sepsis
    c.   Inadequate fluid resuscitation

89

d.   Myoglobinuria


**Answer d.** Cardiogenic shock is very unlikely in a 28 yo man. Sepsis is unlikely only 12 hours after a burn. That leaves inadequate fluid resuscitation and myoglobinuria as the potential sources of the renal failure.

A CVP of 18 would suggest the patient is adequately fluid resuscitated. Thus, myoglobinuria induced ATN is the best answer.


213. Treatment of patients with severe burn injuries and myoglobinuria consists of:
   a.   Broad spectrum antibiotics
   b.   Aggressive inotropic support
   c.   Fluid resuscitation and HCO3- drip
   d.   CVVH to clear the myoglobin


**Answer c.** The best treatment for patients with burn injuries and myoglobinuria is fluid resuscitation and HCO3- to prevent precipitation of the myoglobin.


214. The most common infection in patients with large (> 35%) severe burns is:
   a.   Pneumonia
   b.   Urinary tract infections
   c.   Burn wound sepsis
   d.   Liver abscess


**Answer a.** Although urinary tract infection is the most common infection in surgery patients, pneumonia is the leading cause of infection in patients with severe burn injuries.

Inhalation injury, decreased immunity, fluid resuscitation causing pulmonary edema, and requirement for mechanical ventilation all lead to increased risk for pneumonia. In some series, 60-70% of all patients with large severe burns get pneumonia.

215. The best way to diagnose burn wound sepsis is:
    a. Culture swab of the wound
    b. Biopsy of the wound
    c. Blood cultures
    d. Examination

    **Answer b.** The best way to diagnose infection of a burn wound is to biopsy the burn wound.

216. You are getting ready to place a skin graft on a burn area. A burn wound biopsy shows $10^4$ staph epidermidis/gram of tissue. The next appropriate step in management is:
    a. Nothing
    b. Broad spectrum antibiotics
    c. Vancomycin
    d. Proceed with auto-grafting

    **Answer d.** The diagnosis of a burn wound infection requires $> 10^5$ organisms/gram of tissue, otherwise it is considered colonization.

    If there was an infection present in the burn wound, in addition to starting antibiotics, going ahead with excising the burn wound (and the infection) and placing a porcine allograft is a reasonable option. You would not want to place an autograft in this situation.

217. The most common organism involved in burn wound sepsis is:
    a. Staph aureus
    b. Pseudomonas
    c. Strep viridans
    d. Klebsiella

91

**Answer b.** Pseudomonas is the most common organism involved in burn wound sepsis.


218. Skin grafts survive in the $1^{st}$ 48 hours primary by:
   a. Neovascularization
   b. Reliance on stored glycogen
   c. Gluconeogenesis
   d. Imbibition

**Answer d.** Skin grafts survive by imbibition (osmotic exchange of nutrients) for the $1^{st}$ 48 hours. After that, neovascularization takes over.


219. In comparison of split thickness skin grafts (STSG) to full thickness skin grafts (FTSG), all of the following are true except:
   a. STSG are more likely to survive
   b. FTSG have less wound contraction
   c. FTSG are good for palmar burns
   d. The most common reason for skin graft loss is infection

**Answer d.** STSG are more likely to survive compared to FTSG because they are thinner and more likely to survive the imbibition and early neovascularization periods (harder for imbibition to work with thicker grafts).

FTSG have less wound contraction compared to STSG (good for places like the hand and face).

The most common cause of skin graft loss is seroma (or hematoma) formation underneath the skin graft, which raises it and prevents neovascularization.

220. You bring an intubated 30 yo man with a 60% total body surface burn back to the OR for his 3$^{rd}$ debridement in 3 days and the anesthesiologist gives him succinylcholine instead of the pancuronium which he was receiving in the intensive care unit. Shortly after this, his EKG shows T wave abnormalities, then a widened QRS, and then ventricular fibrillation. You cannot feel a pulse so you start CPR and shock him 3 times without success. The 1$^{st}$ drug you should give for this problem is:

    a. Dantrolene
    b. Calcium gluconate
    c. Methylene blue
    d. Atropine

**Answer b.** Burn patients are at increased risk for hyperkalemia because of myonecrosis and leaking of potassium into the blood stream. This, combined with succinylcholine which causes potassium release when it depolarizes the cell membrane, results in hyperkalemia.

The 1$^{st}$ treatment of choice when hyperkalemia occurs with arrhythmias is Calcium gluconate. This stabilizes the myocardial cell membrane and will help stabilize the arrhythmia.

Dextrose 50% and 10 units of insulin, HCO3-, Kaexylate, dialysis, etc can be used to help treat hyperkalemia.

221. A common complication of silvadene for burns is:
    a. Neutropenia and thrombocytopenia
    b. Acidosis
    c. Hyponatremia and hypochloremia
    d. Hyperkalemia

**Answer a.** Neutropenia and thrombocytopenia are side effects of silvadene.

222. A common complication of sulfamylon for burns is:

93

a. Neutropenia and thrombocytopenia
b. Acidosis
c. Hyponatremia and hypochloremia
d. Hyperkalemia


**Answer b.** Sulfamylon can cause metabolic acidosis from carbonic anhydrase inhibition in the kidney.


223. A common complication of silver nitrate for burns is:
a. Neutropenia and thrombocytopenia
b. Acidosis
c. Hyponatremia and hypochloremia
d. Hyperkalemia


**Answer c.** Silver nitrate can cause hyponatremia, hypochloremia, hypocalcemia, and hypokalemia.

It can also cause methemoglobinemia and is contraindicated in G6PD deficiency patients.

# Head and Neck

224. A 50 yo man has a mass 1 cm anterior to the ear. The mass causes him pain and he has a facial droop. CT of the head shows the tumor is involved in both the deep and superficial portions of the gland. This most likely represents:
   a. Mucoepidermoid carcinoma
   b. Adenoid cystic carcinoma
   c. Pleomorphic adenoma
   d. Warthin's Tumor

   **Answer a.** There are 2 features of this presentation that make the parotid tumor almost certainly malignant. The first is that it invades both the superficial and deep glands (unusual for benign tumors) and the second is that the facial nerve is affected (facial droop).

   Given that this tumor is almost certainly malignant, you have to go with the most common malignant tumor of the parotid, which is mucoepidermoid carcinoma.

225. The nerve involved in the tumor in the above patient is most likely the:
   a. Facial nerve
   b. Glossopharyngeal nerve
   c. Auriculo-temporal nerve
   d. Vagus nerve

   **Answer a.** The facial nerve controls motor function to the face.

226. Treatment of the above tumor (mucoepidermoid carcinoma) will most likely involve:
   a. Superficial parotidectomy
   b. Total parotidectomy
   c. Chemo-XRT only

95

d.   Chemotherapy only


**Answer b.** Initial treatment of the above tumor is total parotidectomy including the facial nerve (because it is already out).

You would also need to figure out whether or not this is a low grade mucoepidermoid carcinoma.

If it is low grade mucoepidermoid, you are done.

If it is high grade mucoepidermoid or any other cell type, you should perform a prophylactic modified radical neck dissection and give post op XRT.


227. The most common benign tumor is:
    a.   Mucoepidermoid carcinoma
    b.   Adenoid cystic carcinoma
    c.   Pleomorphic adenoma
    d.   Warthin's Tumor


**Answer c.** The most common benign tumor is pleomorphic adenoma.


228. The tumor most likely to involve bilateral parotid glands at the time of presentation is:
    a.   Mucoepidermoid carcinoma
    b.   Adenoid cystic carcinoma
    c.   Pleomorphic adenoma
    d.   Warthin's Tumor


**Answer d.** The tumor most likely to involve bilateral parotid glands at the same time is Warthin's tumor.

229. Treatment of most benign parotid tumors involves:
   a. Superficial parotidectomy
   b. Total parotidectomy
   c. Chemo-XRT
   d. Chemotherapy

   **Answer a.** Treatment of most benign parotid tumors involves superficial parotidectomy.

230. Following a parotidectomy, a patient has gustatory sweating. This is most likely caused by:
   a. Recurrent tumor
   b. Cross-innervation of the vagus and sympathetic nerves to the skin
   c. Cross-innervation of the auriculotemporal nerve and sympathetic nerves to the skin
   d. Cross-innervation of the glossopharyngeal nerve and sympathetic nerves to the skin

   **Answer c.** Post-op gustatory sweating is caused by cross-innervation of the auriculotemporal nerve and the sympathetic nerves of the skin.

   This usually goes away but if it is refractory, you can place an alloderm skin graft between the skin nerves and the auriculotemporal nerve.

231. The nerve most likely injured with submandibular resection is:
   a. Vagus
   b. Hypoglossal
   c. Auriculotemporal
   d. Marginal mandibular

   **Answer d.** The nerve most commonly injured with resection of the mandibular gland is the marginal mandibular nerve. This nerve supplies the lower lip and chin.

97

232. Massive bleeding 7 days after tracheostomy is most likely from:
   a. Tracheo-carotid fistula
   b. Tracheo-innominate fistula
   c. Tracheo-aortic fistula
   d. Tracheo-jugular fistula

   **Answer b.** The most common case of massive bleeding following tracheostomy is a tracheo-innominate fistula.

   For this, place your finger through the tracheostomy site and try to compress the innominate artery against the sternum.

   Go to the OR for median sternotomy.

   Ligate and divide the innominate artery (some say place a graft but you are at high risk of infection with this complication).

   Ligation of the innominate artery proximal to the takeoff of the right subclavian usually does not result in any neurological dysfunction due to collateral flow.

233. A 35 yo woman comes in with the chief complaint of tinnitus and hearing loss. You order a head MRI and there is a tumor at the cerebello-pontine angle. The most likely diagnosis is:
   a. Glioma
   b. Glioma multiforme
   c. Neuroma
   d. Meduloblastoma

   **Answer c.** Unsteadiness, tinnitus, and hearing loss are the classic symptoms of an acoustic neuroma. A tumor at the cerebello-pontine almost ensures the diagnosis.

234. A 10 yo boy presents with a cyst and a cyst tract near the angle of his mandible. This cyst has had recurrent infections in it. This cyst most likely connects to the:

a. External auditory canal
b. The tonsilar pillar
c. The nasal septum
d. Thoracic duct

**Answer a.** Type I branchial cleft cysts extend from the angle of the mandible to the external auditory canal.

235. A 10 yo boy presents with a cyst in his lateral neck medial to the anterior border of the sternocleidomastoid muscle. This cyst most likely connects to the:
a. External auditory canal
b. The tonsilar pillar
c. The nasal septum
d. Thoracic duct

**Answer b.** Type II branchial cleft cysts extend from the anterior border of the sternocleidomastoid muscle, through the carotid bifurcation, to the tonsilar pillar.

236. The most common branchial cleft cyst is:
a. Type I
b. Type II
c. Type III
d. Type IV

**Answer b.** The most common branchial cleft cyst is type II.

237. Treatment of branchial cleft cysts involves:
a. antibiotics
b. resection
c. XRT
d. Chemotherapy

**Answer b.** Treatment of branchial cleft cysts involves resection.

238. A 5 yo girl presents with a midline anterior neck mass that moves with tongue protrusion and swallowing. This most likely represents:
   a. Thyroid cancer
   b. Branchial cleft cyst Type I
   c. Branchial cleft cyst Type II
   d. Thyroglossal duct cyst

**Answer d.** A midline anterior neck mass in a child that moves with tongue protrusion and swallowing is classic for a thyroglossal duct cyst. Thyroid CA would appear more lateral as would branchial cleft cysts.

239. Resection of this cyst involves:
   a. removal of the cyst only
   b. removal of the cyst and total thyroidectomy
   c. removal of the cyst along with the hyoid bone
   d. post-op XRT

**Answer c.** Important to remember that you need to resect the hyoid bone (or at least the central portion of it) when resecting these cysts so that they do not recur. This is called the sistrunk procedure.

## Adrenal

240. You take a 35 year old man to the operating room for resection of a pheochromocytoma however after very careful inspection of both adrenal glands, you cannot find the tumor. The most likely location for the missing tumor is:
    a.  Lung
    b.  Liver
    c.  Aortic bifurcation
    d.  Spleen

    **Answer c.** The most common location for an extra-adrenal pheochromocytoma is the Organ of Zuckerkandl which is located at the aortic bifurcation.

    Approximately 10% of all pheochromocytomas are extra-adrenal.

    Extra-adrenal pheochromocytomas are more likely to be malignant compared to adrenal pheochromocytomas.

    Extra-adrenal pheochromocytomas do <u>not</u> make epinephrine.

241. A 20 yo man comes to your office and has a blood pressure of 240/120. He states that he gets headaches sometimes when he lifts. Given the most likely diagnosis, which of the following tests is best for making this diagnosis:
    a.  24 hour urine VMA and metanephrines
    b.  Urine cortisol
    c.  Urine aldosterone
    d.  Serum epinephrine and norepinephrine levels

    **Answer a.** The best test for the diagnosis of pheochromocytoma is a 24 hour urine VMA and metanephrine collection study.

242. The test you order above is suggestive of pheochromocytoma. You order a CT scan of the chest and abdomen but can't find any tumor. The most sensitive test for finding the pheochromocytoma is:
   a. MIBG scan
   b. MRI
   c. PET scan
   d. Angiogram

**Answer a.** The most sensitive test for finding a pheochromocytoma is a MIBG scan (131-meta-iodobenzylguanidine), which is a norepinephrine analogue.

243. MIBG scan in the above patient shows a tumor in the right adrenal. You want to get the patient prepared for surgery by $1^{st}$ prescribing:
   a. Propanolol
   b. Phenoxybenzamine
   c. Dilaudid for headaches
   d. ASA

**Answer b.** The $1^{st}$ drug you should prescribe for this patient is an alpha blocker (phenoxybenzamine or prazosin). Then have them try to hydrate as much as possible. You want to gradually increase the alpha blocker dose until they have slight orthostatic hypotension. This should be done 4 weeks before surgery.

Do <u>not</u> prescribe beta-blockers as the $1^{st}$ drug – this can lead to hypertensive crisis from un-opposed alpha stimulation.

244. For the above patient, in general, beta-blockers are avoided as the $1^{st}$ medication because of the potential for:
   a. Bradycardia
   b. Euphoria
   c. Hypertensive crisis
   d. Poor renal perfusion

**Answer c.** Prescribing beta-blockers as the 1$^{st}$ drug can precipitate hypertensive crisis.

## Thyroid and Parathyroid

245. A 29 yo woman undergoes total thyroidectomy for follicular cell carcinoma. After a coughing episode in the post anesthesia care unit, the patient develops severe respiratory stridor and has bulging of her incision. The most appropriate next step is:
    a.  Albuterol nebulizer
    b.  Heli-ox
    c.  Open the incision at the bedside
    d.  Racemic epinephrine

    **Answer c.** This patient has an obvious hematoma causing her respiratory compromise and you should open her incision to evacuate the hematoma.

246. The most common location for a missed parathyroid gland at re-exploration is:
    a.  Posterior mediastinum
    b.  Anterior mediastinum
    c.  Thymus
    d.  Normal anatomic position

    **Answer d.** The most common location of a missing parathyroid gland at re-op is normal anatomic position.

247. The blood supply to the parathyroid glands is:
    a.  Superior thyroid artery for both glands
    b.  Inferior thyroid artery for both glands
    c.  Superior thyroid artery for the superior glands and the inferior thyroid artery for the inferior glands
    d.  Transverse cervical artery for both glands

    **Answer b.** The blood supply to the superior and inferior parathyroid glands is the inferior thyroid arteries.

104

248. Most common location for an ectopic parathyroid gland is:
    a.  posterior mediastinum
    b.  intra-thyroidal
    c.  esophageal wall
    d.  thymus

**Answer d.** The most common location for an ectopic parathyroid gland is the thymus.

249. Most common cause of hypo-parathyroidism is:
    a.  Previous thyroid surgery
    b.  Radiation therapy
    c.  Chemotherapy
    d.  Malignancy

**Answer a.** The most common cause of hypoparathyroidism is previous thyroid surgery.

250. Parathyroid hormone:
    a.  Increases renal absorption of Ca and increases osteoblastic incorporation of Ca into bone
    b.  Decreases renal absorption of Ca and increases osteoblastic incorporation of Ca into bone
    c.  Increases renal absorption of Ca and increases osteoclastic release of Ca from bone
    d.  Decreases renal absorption of Ca and increases osteoclastic release of Ca from bone

**Answer c.** Parathyroid hormone increases resorption of Ca from the kidney as well as increases osteoclastic release of Ca from bone.

105

Additionally, it increases vitamin D hydroxylation in the kidney which eventually results in increased Ca resorption from the gut.

Parathyroid hormone causes secretion of PO4 in the kidney.

251. Which of the flowing lab values are most consistent with primary hyperparathyroidism?
   a. Cl 105, phosphate 3 and elevated renal cAMP
   b. Cl 105, phosphate 4 and elevated renal cAMP
   c. Cl 107, phosphate 3 and decreased renal cAMP
   d. Cl 106, phosphate 4 and decreased renal cAMP

   **Answer a.** Primary hyperparathyroidism is associated with an elevated PTH, elevated Ca, elevated renal cAMP (effect of PTH on the PTH receptor in the kidney), and a Cl:PO4 ratio > 33.

   The half-life of PTH is 18 minutes.

252. The most common cause of persistent primary hyper-parathyroidism is:
   a. Parathyroid cancer
   b. Parathyroid hyperplasia
   c. Missed adenoma
   d. New adenoma

   **Answer c.** The most common cause of persistent hyperparathyroidism is missed adenoma. Approximately 5% will have multiple adenomas at the time of surgery for hyperparathyroidism.

253. A 30 yo woman recently diagnosed with MEN I syndrome develops confusion, somnolence, and a shortened QT on EKG. The next appropriate step is:

106

a. Alpha-blockade
b. Beta-blockade
c. Calcium
d. Intravenous fluids and lasix

**Answer d.** MEN I syndrome includes parathyroid hyperplasia, pancreatic tumors, and pituitary tumors. Of these, only hypercalcemia is associated with confusion, somnolence, and a shortened QT on EKG (although a large prolactinoma could cause just the mental status changes).

Given the likely culprit is hyperparathyroidism, hypercalcemia is the most likely diagnosis.

Treatment for hypercalcemia is IVF's (normal saline at 200-300 cc/hr – <u>NO lactated ringers</u> which contains Ca) and lasix (not thiazide diuretics which cause Ca resorption).

Just to re-state: lactated ringers and thiazide diuretics are contra-indicated in patients with hypercalcemia.

254. A 50 yo woman comes in with the chief complaint of a nodule in her neck. You get a TSH and a T3, both of which are normal. The most appropriate next step in management is:
    a. Thyroid lobectomy
    b. Total thyroidectomy
    c. Ultrasound and FNA
    d. Neck MRI

**Answer c.** After getting baseline TFT's (some surgeons wouldn't even do those), you should get an ultrasound and FNA in the office.

255. Ultrasound on the above patient reveals a 1.2 cm mass. You get the pathology back on the FNA and it shows follicular cells. The most appropriate next step in management is:
    a. Thyroid lobectomy

107

    b.   Nothing
    c.   Neck CT
    d.   Neck MRI

**Answer a.** Follicular cells on FNA has been shown to result in follicular cell CA in 10% of patients. You need to perform a thyroid lobectomy and get a definitive diagnosis.

256. You take the above patient to the operating room and perform a thyroid lobectomy. Pathology shows this is a 1.9 cm follicular cell carcinoma. The most appropriate next step is:
    a.   Completion total thyroidectomy
    b.   Close
    c.   Post op chemotherapy
    d.   Post-op XRT

**Answer a.** Thyroid CA with a size > 1 cm requires total thyroidectomy.

Indications for total thyroidectomy include:

Tumor > 1 cm
Extra-thyroidal disease (capsular invasion, clinical or positive nodal disease, or metastases)
Multicentric DZ
History of XRT

257. The above patient also had palpable lymph nodes in her neck on physical exam prior to surgery. The most appropriate management is:
    a.   Cherry pick the lymph nodes out of the neck
    b.   Radical neck dissection
    c.   Modified radical neck dissection
    d.   Post op XRT

**Answer c.** Patients with thyroid CA and clinically positive lymph nodes should undergo total thyroidectomy and modified radical neck dissection.

Indications for modified radical neck dissection:

Extra-thyroidal DZ (capsule invasion, clinical or positive nodal DZ or mets)

258. Post-operatively the above opera singer has a loss of voice pitch. This is most likely due to injury of the:
    a. Superior laryngeal nerve
    b. Recurrent laryngeal nerve
    c. Vagus nerve
    d. Glossopharyngeal nerve

**Answer a.** Loss of pitch is most consistent with superior laryngeal nerve injury.

259. Instead of the above, post-operatively this patient has a hoarse voice. This is most likely due to injury of the:
    a. Superior laryngeal nerve
    b. Recurrent laryngeal nerve
    c. Vagus nerve
    d. Glossopharyngeal nerve

**Answer b.** Hoarseness is most consistent with recurrent laryngeal nerve injury.

260. After total thyroidectomy and modified radical neck dissection in a patient w/ thyroid CA (1.9 cm follicular cell CA and positive nodes on final pathology), post-operatively this patient should also undergo:
    a. I-131 therapy
    b. XRT

109

    c.   Chemotherapy (5-FU)
    d.   Tamoxifen therapy

**Answer a.** I-131 is a very effective treatment for disseminated thyroid CA.

Indications for I-131 treatment include:

Tumor > 1cm
Extra-thyroidal DZ (capsule invasion, positive nodal DZ
    or metastases)

261. Following I-131, the most effective way of suppressing the growth of any residual follicular or papillary thyroid cancer is:
    a.   Thyroid hormone replacement
    b.   Daily calcium
    c.   Daily phosphate replacement
    d.   Daily potassium

**Answer a.** Thyroid hormone replacement following resection for thyroid CA is a very effective tumor suppressor adjunct. By giving thyroid hormone, you effectively suppress TSH production and inhibit tumor growth.

262. Which of the following lab values is most effective at picking up recurrent papillary or follicular thyroid cancer?
    a.   TSH
    b.   TRH
    c.   Thyroglobulin
    d.   Transferrin

**Answer c.** Following serum thyroglobulin levels after total thyroidectomy is a very effective way of detecting recurrence.

263. Post-operatively, a patient undergoing a difficult total thyroidectomy has severe respiratory stridor and impending respiratory arrest immediately after extubation in the post-anesthesia care unit. She does not have any signs of hematoma. The most effective way of airway access is:
    a. Re-intubation
    b. Open the wound and place emergent tracheostomy
    c. Take her back to the OR for re-exploration
    d. Racemic epinephrine

    **Answer b.** Given the clinical scenario, this patient likely suffered bilateral RLN injury.

    Trying to intubate a patient with bilateral RLN injury and medialization of both cords is very difficult. The best option is emergent tracheostomy through the collar incision (which you performed for the thyroidectomy).

264. All of the following are true of the recurrent laryngeal nerve except:
    a. The right RLN runs more lateral than the left RLN
    b. The right RLN is more likely to be non-recurrent compared to the left
    c. The right RLN wraps around the innominate artery and the left RLN wraps around the aorta
    d. The recurrent laryngeal nerve innervates the cricothyroid muscle

    **Answer d.** The right recurrent laryngeal nerve runs more lateral than the left recurrent laryngeal nerve.

    The right RLN wraps around the innominate artery before ascending into the neck. The right RLN is much more likely to be non-recurrent compared to the left RLN.

    The left RLN wraps around the aorta before ascending into the neck.

111

The RLN's are the motor supply to all of the larynx <u>except</u> the cricothyroid muscle.

The cricothyroid muscle is innervated by the superior laryngeal nerve.

In terms of a <u>non-recurrent</u> recurrent laryngeal nerve, a replaced right subclavian artery coming off the descending aorta is one of the most common reasons for a <u>non-recurrent</u> recurrent laryngeal nerve.

265. A 31 yo woman is 21 ½ weeks pregnant with her 1$^{st}$ pregnancy and has severe tremors, tachycardia, and sweating. Her endocrinologist makes the diagnosis of hyperthyroidism and starts her on propylthiouracil, however the patient continues to have tachycardia, tremors and sweating. The endocrinologist wants your input on what to do next. You advise the endocrinologist that the most appropriate next step is:
    a. Propanolol
    b. I-131
    c. Thyroidectomy
    d. Methimazole

**Answer c.** The problem in this patient is that you cannot use either I-131 or methimazole because of their teratogenic effects.

I-131 will ablate the fetal thyroid.

Methimazole causes cretinism (stunted physical and mental growth due to hypothyroidism).

Propylthiouracil is safe because it does not cross the placenta.

You could use a beta-blocker, but you would still have hyperthyroidism (albeit with a lower heart rate) and an increased risk of stillbirth.

Also, beta-blockers are contra-indicated in the 3<sup>rd</sup> trimester of pregnancy as they have been associated with fetal growth retardation.

266. The most appropriate initial treatment for thyroid storm includes:
    a.   Dantrolene
    b.   Phenylephrine
    c.   Emergent thyroidectomy
    d.   Propanolol

**Answer d.** Beta-blockers are used in the initial treatment of thyroid storm.

Treatment of thyroid storm includes:

- Beta-blockers (esmolol drip usually)
- Lugol's (KI)
- Propylthiouracil
- Cooling blankets
- Oxygen
- Glucose
- Fluid
- Steroids (cortisol 100 mg Q 8)

267. The Wolff Chaikoff effect describes:
    a.   Effect of a beta-blocker therapy during thyroid crisis
    b.   Iodide inhibition of T3 and T4 release
    c.   The effect of cooling the patient in thyroid storm
    d.   The mechanism of propylthiouracil on the thyroid gland

**Answer b.** High doses of iodine (Lugol's solution, potassium iodide) inhibit TSH action on thyroid and inhibits organic coupling of iodide to tyrosine, resulting in less T3 and T4 release.

268. The mechanism of propylthiouracil is:
    a.  preventing uptake of iodide
    b.  inhibition of peroxidases and iodide binding
    c.  blockade of the T3 and T4 receptor
    d.  binding of free T3 and T4

**Answer b.**

PTU inhibits peroxidases, which connects iodine to tyrosine to form di-iodo-tyrosine (T4) and mono-iodo-tyrosine (T3).

PTU also blocks the conversion of T4 to T3 in the periphery (also peroxidases).

269. Which of the following is characteristic of MEN I:
    a.  Parathyroid hyperplasia, pancreatic tumors, pituitary tumors
    b.  Parathyroid hyperplasia, medullary carcinoma of the thyroid, and pheochromocytoma
    c.  medullary carcinoma of the thyroid, pheochromocytoma, marfanoid habitus, mucosal neuroma
    d.  Von recklinghausen's Disease

**Answer a.** MEN I consists of parathyroid hyperplasia, pancreatic tumors (gastrinoma is the most common for this syndrome), and pituitary tumors (prolactinoma is the most common for this syndrome).

Note that insulinoma is the most common endocrine pancreatic tumor overall (but not in the MEN sub-group).

The 1st part to become symptomatic is parathyroid hyperplasia.

The major morbidity and mortality of the syndrome is from pancreatic tumors.

You need to correct the parathyroid hyperplasia 1st with MEN I if synchronous tumors present.

270. Which of the following is characteristic of MEN IIa:
    a.  Parathyroid hyperplasia, pancreatic tumors, pituitary tumors
    b.  Parathyroid hyperplasia, medullary carcinoma of the thyroid, and pheochromocytoma
    c.  Medullary carcinoma of the thyroid, pheochromocytoma, marfanoid habitus, mucosal neuroma
    d.  Von recklinghausen's Disease

**Answer b.** MEN IIa consists of parathyroid hyperplasia, medullary carcinoma of the thyroid, and pheochromocytoma.

The $1^{st}$ part to become symptomatic is medullary carcinoma of the thyroid (diarrhea from the calcitonin).

The major morbidity and mortality is from medullary carcinoma of the thyroid.

The pheochromocytoma needs to be treated $1^{st}$ if synchronous tumors are present (these are usually benign).


271. Which of the following is characteristic of MEN IIb:
    a.  Parathyroid hyperplasia, pancreatic tumors, pituitary tumors
    b.  Parathyroid hyperplasia, medullary carcinoma of the thyroid, and pheochromocytoma
    c.  medullary carcinoma of the thyroid, pheochromocytoma, marfanoid habitus, mucosal neuroma
    d.  Von recklinghausen's Disease

**Answer c.** MEN IIb consists of medullary carcinoma of the thyroid, pheochromocytoma, marfanoid habitus and mucosal neuromas.

The $1^{st}$ part to become symptomatic is medullary carcinoma of the thyroid (diarrhea from the calcitonin).

115

The major morbidity and mortality is from medullary carcinoma of the thyroid.

The pheochromocytoma needs to be treated $1^{st}$ if synchronous tumors are present (these are usually benign).

Medullary carcinoma in MEN IIb is more aggressive than MEN IIa.

272. Which of the following is most consistent with primary hyperparathyroidism?
    a.  Ca 11, PTH 200, elevated urine Ca
    b.  Ca 8, PTH 200, elevated urine Ca, serum creatnine 7
    c.  Ca 11, PTH 40, low urine calcium
    d.  Ca 8, PTH  35, normal urine calcium

**Answer a.**

Primary hyperparathyroidism is associated with:

- Autonomously elevated PTH (nl 10-60 pg/ml)
- Elevated serum Ca (nl 8.5-10.5)
- Elevated (70%) or normal (30%) urine Ca

273. Which of the following is most consistent with familial hypercalcemic, hypocalciuria?
    a.  Ca 11, PTH 200, elevated urine Ca
    b.  Ca 8, PTH 200, elevated urine Ca, serum creatnine 7
    c.  Ca 11, PTH 40, low urine calcium
    d.  Ca 8, PTH  35, normal urine calcium

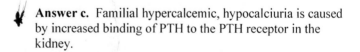

**Answer c.** Familial hypercalcemic, hypocalciuria is caused by increased binding of PTH to the PTH receptor in the kidney.

Clinically, familial hypercalcemic, hypocalciuria is associated w/:

Normal PTH (or slightly elevated)
Elevated serum Ca (only to 11 or so)
❋ Low urine Ca (this is the key finding)

NO parathyroidectomy in these patients.

274. Which of the following is most consistent with secondary hyperparathyroidism:
    a. Ca 11, PTH 200, elevated urine Ca
    b. Ca 8, PTH 200, elevated urine Ca, serum creatnine 7
    c. Ca 11, PTH 40, low urine calcium
    d. Ca 8, PTH  45, normal urine calcium

**Answer b.** Secondary hyperparathyroidism occurs primarily in dialysis patients who have chronic loss of Ca (other diseases where you have chronic loss of calcium can also cause the problem).

Clinically, secondary hypoparathyroidism is associated with:
➤ Elevated PTH
➤ Normal serum Ca

It is unusual to have to operate on patients with renal associated secondary hyperparathyroidism.

The most common indication for operation in patients with secondary hyperparathyroidism is bone pain as a result of Ca resorption.

## Breast

275. All of the following are characteristic of male breast cancer except:
    a.  Association with the BRCA gene
    b.  Majority are estrogen receptor positive
    c.  Often get lobular breast cancer
    d.  Risk factors include Klinefelter's and steroid use

**Answer c.** Male breast cancer represents less than 1% of all breast cancer. It is almost exclusively ductal carcinoma, the vast majority are estrogen receptor positive, and many of them have pectoral involvement because of delayed diagnosis.

- Risk factors include steroids, XRT, family history, Klinefelter's Syndrome.

Males do not get lobular carcinoma of the breast.

Treatment usually involves modified radical mastectomy, post-op chemotherapy (if > 1 cm or positive nodes) and Tamoxifen (if receptor positive).

276. All of the following are true of Tamoxifen except:
    a.  1% risk of blood clots
    b.  Dose is 1 mg/d for 5 years
    c.  0.1% risk of endometrial CA
    d.  Need to have positive ER or PR receptors to have benefit

**Answer b.** There is a 1% risk of DVT or PE and a 0.1% risk of endometrial CA with Tamoxifen.

Positive receptors (progesterone or estrogen) are required for effective treatment.

The dose of Tamoxifen is 20 mg/day for 5 years.

277. All of the following are true of Tamoxifen except:
   a.   Dose is 20 mg/day for 5 years
   b.   Reduces annual odds of breast cancer recurrence by approximately 50%
   c.   Reduces the annual odds of death from breast cancer by 25%
   d.   Is effective chemotherapy in patients with negative receptors


   **Answer d.** Tamoxifen reduces annual odds of breast cancer recurrence by approximately 50%. It also reduces the annual odds of death from breast cancer by 25%

   Tamoxifen is not effective in receptor negative patients.


278. A 46 yo woman undergoes breast biopsy and the pathology comes back as cystosarcoma phyllodes. You find no evidence of metastatic disease. The most appropriate management is:
   a.   Modified radical mastectomy
   b.   Lumpectomy and axillary lymph node dissection
   c.   Radical mastectomy
   d.   Wide local excision


   **Answer d.** Cystosarcoma phyllodes is a sarcoma. Sarcomas rarely have metastases to the lymph nodes. Treatment of this lesion consists of wide local excision. You could also perform simple mastectomy.


279. A 50 yo woman comes to clinic and has a 4 cm ductal carcinoma on mammography. You perform a physical exam on the patient and you notice the lymph nodes in her axilla are fixed and matted. Work up for metastatic disease is negative. This patients clinical stage is:
   a.   Stage IB
   b.   Stage IIA
   c.   Stage IIB
   d.   Stage IIIA

119

**Answer d.** A 4 cm cancer is T2 and fixed or matted nodes is N2. Thus, this patient is T2N2M0, which is stage IIIa.

Stage I – T1, N0, M0
Stage IIa – T0-1, N1, M0 or T2, N0, M0
Stage IIb – T2, N1, M0 or T3, N0, M0
Stage IIIa – T0-3, N2, M0 or T3, N1-2, M0
Stage IIIb – any T4 or N3 tumors
Stage IV – M1

280. All of the following are surgical options for this patient except:
    a. Lumpectomy and axillary lymph node dissection
    b. Modified radical mastectomy
    c. Lumpectomy and sentinel lymph node biopsy
    d. Quadrectomy and axillary lymph node dissection

**Answer c.** Patients with clinically positive nodes are not candidates for sentinel lymph node biopsy.

281. While performing a modified radical mastectomy in the above patient, you cut the long thoracic nerve. Post-operatively, this patient is most likely to have:
    a. Weak adduction
    b. Winged scapula
    c. Weak abduction
    d. Paralyzed diaphragm

**Answer b.** The long thoracic nerve innervates the serratus anterior muscle. Laceration of this nerve will cause a winged scapula.

282. While performing a modified radical mastectomy in the above
patient, you cut the thoracodorsal nerve. Post-operatively, this
patient is most likely to have:
   a.   Weak adduction
   b.   Winged scapula
   c.   Weak abduction
   d.   Paralyzed diaphragm

**Answer a.** The thoracodorsal nerve innervates the latissimus
dorsi muscle. Injury to this nerve will result in weak
adduction (and inability to do a pull-up).

283. After modified radical mastectomy in the above patient, pathology
shows that the tumor is 4 cm and 6 lymph nodes are positive.
Estrogen receptors are positive but progesterone receptors are
negative. The most appropriate post-op management is:
   a.   XRT and chemotherapy (Adriamycin and
         cyclophosphamide: followed by Tamoxifen)
   b.   Tamoxifen only
   c.   XRT only
   d.   Chemotherapy (Adriamycin and cyclophosphamide) and
         Tamoxifen

**Answer a.**
Indications for XRT after modified radical mastectomy are:

   Skin or chest wall involvement
   Positive margins
   · Tumor >5 cm (T3)
   ، Inflammatory CA
   ، Advanced Nodal Disease - > 4 nodes positive,
         extracapsular invasion, fixed axillary (N2) or internal
         mammary (N3)

This patient also needs chemotherapy (CMF or AC for
   positive nodes or a tumor > 1 cm)

This patient should also receive Tamoxifen (for progesterone
   or estrogen receptor positive tumors).

121

284. A 56 yo woman has a 2 cm ductal carcinoma on core needle biopsy and negative nodes on clinical exam. You decide to perform a sentinel lymph node biopsy using lymphazurin blue dye. You perform the lumpectomy but after 3 hours of searching you cannot find any blue nodes. The next appropriate step is:
   a. Modified radical mastectomy
   b. Close
   c. Randomly sample nodes
   d. Formal axillary lymph nodes dissection

   **Answer d.** If you cannot find any blue nodes, you cannot accurately stage the patient. You need to perform an axillary lymph node dissection.

285. In the above patient, instead of finding no nodes, you find 3 blue nodes. The next appropriate step is:
   a. Modified radical mastectomy
   b. Take all the blue nodes
   c. Randomly sample nodes
   d. Formal axillary lymph nodes dissection

   **Answer b.** You should take all of the blue nodes. Typically, with sentinel lymph node biopsy you find 1-3 nodes.

286. Instead of lymphazurin blue dye in the above patient, you decide to use technetium labeled sulfur colloid. You find one node that has a count of 1500, another node with a count of 200, and 4 other nodes with counts of 10-20. The most appropriate management is:
   a. Resect the node with the highest count only
   b. Resect all nodes with any gamma activity
   c. Perform formal axillary lymph node dissection
   d. Resect the highest count node and any nodes 10% or greater than that node

**Answer d.** In general, you should resect the lymph node with the highest count and any lymph node greater than 10% of the highest count lymph node.

287. In the above patient, in addition to the previous lymph node findings, the supraclavicular area has a count of 1000 which does not seem to be from the axilla. You should now:
    a. Continue with resecting the highest count node and any nodes 10% or greater than that node *only* in the axilla
    b. Formal axillary lymph node dissection
    c. Continue with resecting the highest count node and any nodes 10% or greater than that node in addition to exploring the supraclavicular area
    d. Resect the node with the highest gamma count only

**Answer c.** Unusually, you find a node that is hot which is outside the area you were expecting. You need to go after that node for staging purposes.

288. Contraindications to sentinel lymph node biopsy include all of the following except:
    a. pregnancy
    b. multicentric primary disease
    c. neoadjuvant therapy
    d. lobular carcinoma

**Answer d.**

Contraindications to sentinel lymph node biopsy include all of the following:

- Pregnancy
- Multi-centric disease
- Neoadjuvant therapy
- Advanced disease
- Palpable nodes

· Previous axillary dissection

Large tumor (> 2.5 cm) – blocks the lymphatics (relative)
Tumor has already been taken out (relative)

289. All of the following are true of the BRCA gene except:
  a.   BRCA gene with a family history of breast cancer equates with a 60% lifetime risk of breast cancer
  b.   BRCA I gene equates with an ovarian cancer risk of 40% (lifetime)
  c.   BRCA II gene equates with an ovarian cancer risk of 10% (lifetime)
  d.   BRCA II gene equates with a male breast cancer risk of 1% (lifetime)

**Answer d.** BRCA II is associated with a 10% male breast cancer risk (lifetime).

BRCA gene + family history = 60% lifetime risk of breast CA (autosomal dominant)

BRCA I
    Ovarian CA – 40% lifetime risk
    Male Breast CA – 1% lifetime risk

BRCA II
    Ovarian CA – 10% lifetime risk
    Male Breast CA – 10% lifetime risk

Of note, when the BRCA gene was originally discovered, it was thought that the lifetime incidence of breast cancer was going to be 90%. This greatly overestimated the true risk and follow-up studies have shown the true lifetime risk of breast cancer in BRCA positive patients with a family history of breast cancer to be 60%.

290. All of the following are true of breast cancer receptors except:
  a.   Progesterone receptor positive tumors have a better prognosis than receptor negative tumors

124

b. Estrogen receptor positive tumors have a better prognosis than receptor negative tumors
c. HER receptor positive tumors have a better prognosis
d. neu receptor positive tumors have a worse prognosis

**Answer c.** Tumors containing the HER receptor have a worse prognosis. These patients can be treated with Herceptin (antibody to the HER receptor).

Estrogen and progesterone positive tumors have the best prognosis.

Neu receptor positive tumors have a worse prognosis.

Progesterone receptor positive tumors have a slightly better prognosis than estrogen positive tumors.

 $P > E$

291. All of the following are true of lobular carcinoma except:
a. Form extensive calcifications
b. Often multicentric
c. Represents approximately 10% of all breast CA
d. Has an increased risk of bilateral involvement

**Answer a.** Lobular carcinomas do not have calcification.

They are at increased risk for multicentricity and bilateral tumors.

Lobular breast cancers represent 10% of all breast cancer.

292. A 60 yo woman has a palpable node in her axilla. You get a bilateral mammogram and CXR which are both negative. You decide to excise the node and you find adenocarcinoma that is positive for estrogen receptors. The most appropriate next step is:
a. Chemotherapy (Adriamycin and cyclophosphamide)
b. XRT
c. Modified radical mastectomy

d.   Sentinel lymph node biopsy


**Answer c.**  Occult breast cancer can present as an enlarged lymph node in the axilla.  With the finding of breast CA in the axillary node, you should perform a modified radical mastectomy on the same side.  About 70% of the time, you will find breast cancer in the breast after resection.

Instead of performing an excisional biopsy of the node, you could have performed a core needle biopsy.


293. All of the following are contraindications to lumpectomy and XRT except:
   a.   Pregnancy
   b.   Multiple primaries
   c.   Large tumor
   d.   Previous XRT


**Answer c.**

Contraindications to XRT includes:

   Scleroderma (results in severe fibrosis and necrosis)
   Previous XRT
   SLE (relative)
   Active rheumatoid arthritis (relative)
   Pregnancy


294. A 63 yo woman undergoes lumpectomy and axillary lymph node dissection for a T2N1M0 ductal carcinoma.  Six months later, she feels a nodule underneath the suture line.  You get an FNA and it comes back ductal carcinoma.  The most appropriate next step is:
   a.   Repeat lumpectomy including the lump
   b.   Sentinel lymph node biopsy
   c.   XRT
   d.   Modified radical mastectomy

**Answer d.** Treatment for breast cancer recurrence after lumpectomy is modified radical mastectomy.

There is a 2-3% chance of recurrence after appropriate lumpectomy.

295. Lymphazurin blue dye has been associated with what type of hypersensitivity reaction?
    a. Type I
    b. Type II
    c. Type III
    d. Type IV

**Answer a.** Type I hypersensitivity reaction occurs in 1% of patients receiving lymphazurin blue dye.

296. All of the following are true of an axillary lymph node dissection except:
    a. The superior border is the axillary vein
    b. The medial border is the chest wall
    c. The lateral border is the thoracodorsal pedicle
    d. The anterior border is the pectoralis minor muscle

**Answer c.**

Axillary Lymph Node Dissection:
     Superior border – axillary vein
     Medial border – chest wall (watch for long thoracic nerve)
     Lateral border – skin flap
     Anterior border – pectoralis minor muscle
     Posterior border – latissimus dorsi (watch for thoracodorsal nerve)

127

297. The most commonly injured nerve after MRM is:
    a.  Long thoracic
    b.  Thoracodorsal
    c.  Phrenic
    d.  Intercostal brachiocutaneous

**Answer d.** The most commonly injured nerve after modified radical mastectomy is the intercostal brachiocutaneous nerve. Injury to this nerve causes numbness in the axillary area.

298. A 56 yo woman with no PMHx presents to your office with a weepy, scaly like lesion on her right nipple. You perform a formal H and P. What is the most appropriate next step?
    a.  Bilateral Mammogram
    b.  Unilateral Mammogram
    c.  Core needle biopsy
    d.  Find needle aspirate

**Answer a.** The 1$^{st}$ step in any patient over the age of 30 with a suspected breast problem is to get a bilateral mammogram.

299. Mammogram in the above patient is normal. The most appropriate next step is:
    a.  Modified radical mastectomy
    b.  Simple mastectomy
    c.  Wedge biopsy
    d.  XRT

**Answer c.** Hard to tell what this is going to be. Could be Paget's Disease or it could be an inflammatory carcinoma, or a dermatologic skin problem. Need to get a biopsy of the skin and breast tissue to figure it out.

300. Pathology for the above patient shows Paget cells and Ductal Carcinoma In Situ. The most appropriate next step is:
    a.  Modified radical mastectomy
    b.  Simple mastectomy (including the nipple areolar complex)
    c.  Lumpectomy and axillary lymph node biopsy
    d.  XRT

**Answer b.** The treatment of Paget's disease and an underlying ductal carcinoma in situ is simple mastectomy (including the nipple areolar complex).

Typically, a simple mastectomy leaves the nipple-areolar complex but in patients with Paget's, the nipple areolar complex is involved in the disease and needs to be resected.

Of note, patients with Paget's Disease of the Breast may have either an underlying ductal carcinoma in situ or a ductal carcinoma.

301. You perform a simple mastectomy with resection of the nipple-areolar complex in the above patient. While you are closing, pathology calls and says there is a 1 cm ductal carcinoma in the specimen. There is a 1 cm margin around the tumor. The most appropriate next step is:
    a.  Finish closing
    b.  Sentinel lymph node biopsy
    c.  Formal axillary lymph node dissection
    d.  Chest wall resection

**Answer c.** You need to perform an axillary lymph node dissection to properly stage the patient.

## Thoracic

302. In a normal person sitting up, all of the following are true of ventilation perfusion ratio except:
   a. V/Q ratio is greatest at the apex
   b. V/Q ratio is lowest at the bases
   c. When supine for prolonged periods, V/Q ratio changes
   d. The V/Q ratio does not change with posture

**Answer d.** The ventilation perfusion ratio is highest in the apex (alveoli are the most open in the apex and gravity tends to make most of the blood flow go into the lower lobes) and lowest in the bases in a patient who is sitting upright.

When patients are supine for prolonged periods, the posterior portions of the lungs tend to collapse and again gravity tends to make blood go posteriorly. Also, the anterior portions of the lung tend to be more expanded, and thus more open alveoli. Thus, the V/Q ratio changes in patients who are in a supine position for a prolonged period of time.

In severely ill patients, one method of recruiting new alveoli is to transition between prone and supine positioning, which helps keep the alveoli maximally open.

303. Which lung cancer is most likely to be associated with a paraneoplastic syndrome?
   a. Small cell lung CA
   b. Adenocarcinoma
   c. Squamous cell CA
   d. Large cell CA

**Answer a.** Small cell carcinoma is most commonly involved in paraneoplastic syndromes (ACTH and ADH).

Squamous cell carcinoma is associated with PTH-rp release.

130

304. The most common structure involved in thoracic outlet syndrome
is:
a. The subclavian artery
b. The subclavian vein
 c. The brachial plexus
d. The sympathetic chain ganglia

**Answer c.** The brachial plexus is the most common structure
involved in thoracic outlet syndrome.

305. A chylothorax is most common in the left chest after which of the
following procedures:
a. CEA
b. Ivor Lewis esophagectomy
c. Aortic arch aneurysm repair near the left subclavian
artery
d. CABG

**Answer c.** The thoracic duct runs along the right side of the
chest until the T4-T5 vertebra and then it crosses over to the
left side.

Chylothorax can occur on the right side following an Ivor
Lewis esophagectomy, which involves an abdominal incision
and right thoracotomy. It would be unusual, however for this
to occur on the left side after an Ivor Lewis esophagectomy.

Chylothorax can occur after a CEA (the thoracic duct goes up
into the neck a ways before inserting at the junction of the
jugular and innominate veins). This, however, is pretty
unusual and the chyle leak would likely be in the neck.

Chylothorax is pretty rare after CABG because you are
working anterior to the thoracic duct.

Distal aortic arch procedures occur around the thoracic duct
where it has crossed over to the left side and could present
with a left sided chylothorax.

131

306. A chylothorax is most common in the right chest after which of the following procedures:
   a. CEA
   b. Ivor Lewis esophagectomy
   c. Distal aortic arch procedure near the left subclavian artery takeoff
   d. CABG

**Answer b.** Of the procedures listed, chylothorax in the right chest is most common after an Ivor Lewis esophagectomy.

307. The structure most commonly resected for thoracic outlet syndrome is:
   a. Resection of the $1^{st}$ rib
   b. Resection of the $2^{nd}$ rib
   c. Resection of the clavicle
   d. The spinous process of C8

**Answer a.** Key components of treating thoracic outlet syndrome are resection of the $1^{st}$ rib and any cervical ribs.

308. With thoracic outlet syndrome involving the brachial plexus, the most common nerve distribution is:
   a. C2-C3
   b. C5-C6
   c. C8-T1
   d. T3-T4

**Answer c.** The most common part of the brachial plexus involved in thoracic outlet syndrome is C8-T1. This is the lowest portion of the brachial plexus and the part most likely to rub on the $1^{st}$ rib.

309. What percentage of patients have complete resolution of their symptoms after repair of thoracic outlet syndrome?
   a.  100%
   b.  80%
   c.  60%
   d.  40%

   **Answer c.**  Only about 60% of patients have complete resolution of their symptoms after repair.

310. A 24 yo college pitcher comes to the emergency room with acute pain and swelling in his right arm.  You order an ultrasound and there is clot in the subclavian vein.  The next appropriate step is:
   a.  Thrombolytic therapy
   b.  Catheter embolectomy
   c.  Resection of the 1$^{st}$ rib
   d.  Resection of the subclavian vein and reconstruction with an 10 mm Gortex graft

   **Answer a.**  Paget von Schrotter's disease is acute thrombosis of the subclavian vein.  Classically, it presents in pitchers, or patients who have a lot of strenuous repetitive motion in the arm.

   The initial treatment is thrombolytic therapy to open up the vein.

   ● It is a little controversial on what to do next.  Seems like the tendency is to go ahead with 1$^{st}$ rib resection during the same admission and not wait for a repeat episode.

311. During a supra-clavicular approach for thoracic outlet syndrome, the phrenic nerve is located:
   a.  Anterior to the anterior scalene muscle
   b.  Posterior to the anterior scalene muscle
   c.  Anterior to the middle scalene muscle
   d.  Posterior to the middle scalene muscle

**Answer a.** The phrenic nerve is located anterior to the anterior scalene muscle.

312. During a supra-clavicular approach for thoracic outlet syndrome, the long thoracic nerve is located:
    a.  Anterior to the anterior scalene muscle
    b.  Posterior to the anterior scalene muscle
    c.  Anterior to the middle scalene muscle
    d.  Posterior to the middle scalene muscle

    **Answer d.** The long thoracic nerve is located posterior to the middle scalene muscle.

313. A 48 yo male who drinks a case a beer per day develops nausea and vomits. Following this, the patient develops severe chest pain and is brought to the emergency room. The time from the vomiting episode to the time he arrives at the ER is 5 hours. He is able to communicate although he is obviously intoxicated. His BP is 100/50 and has a HR of 110 so you get 2 intravenous lines is him and give him a fluid bolus. You get a CXR and it shows a left effusion and a pneumothorax. What is the most sensitive test for this patient's likely condition?
    a.  Abdominal CT
    b.  Chest CT
    c.  Angiogram
    d.  Gastrograffin swallow, followed by thin barium swallow

    **Answer d.** Although a chest/abd CT scan with oral and IV contrast is a reasonable screen, it is not as sensitive as a swallow for the diagnosis of Boerhaave's Syndrome.

314. The most common location for the above problem is:
    a.  The left posterior lower esophagus

    b.   The left posterior middle esophagus
    c.   The upper stomach
    d.   The left posterior upper esophagus

**Answer a.** The most common location for a Boerhaave's rupture of the esophagus is the left posterior, lower esophagus. Boerhaave's usually perforate into the left chest.

315. You decide to explore this patient. What is the best operative approach?
    a.   Right thoracotomy
    b.   Left thoracotomy
    c.   Thoracoabdominal incision
    d.   Laparotomy

**Answer b.** The best approach for repair of a Boerhaave's laceration in the lower esophagus is left thoracotomy.

If this lesion were to present in the middle or upper 1/3 of the thoracic esophagus, you would go through the right chest.

316. You open the patient and find gastric contents in his chest and notice some of it coming through the esophagus. You wash the contents out of the chest. The most appropriate next step is:
    a.   Place a chest tube and close
    b.   Perform a myotomy
    c.   Full thickness bites through the esophagus where you see the fluid coming out
    d.   Esophagectomy

**Answer b.** Be careful here. After washing out the vomited material, you need to perform a myotomy to see the extent of the injury in the mucosa. Classically, the mucosal injury will extend farther than the muscle injury. So what you see at first glance is <u>not</u> the full extent of the injury.

Esophagectomy would not really be indicated in this scenario as it hasn't been that long since the perforation occurred (5 hours) and gross mediastinitis is unlikely.

Esophagectomy is indicated when the esophagus is too badly damaged or when there is such severe mediastinitis that the esophagus cannot be salvaged. These are more likely to occur with delayed presentation.

317. A 50 yo woman presents to your office with the chief complaint of having trouble swallowing down food. What is the most appropriate 1$^{st}$ test in this patient?
    a. EGD
    b. Chest CT
    c. Barium swallow
    d. Abdominal CT

**Answer c.** The best initial test for dysphagia or odynophagia is a barium swallow.

EGD and CT scan are not as sensitive as the barium swallow in picking up abnormalities.

318. You get a barium swallow on the above patient and it shows a dilated proximal esophagus which ends in a bird's beak tapering. This is most consistent with:
    a. Esophageal CA
    b. Diffuse esophageal spasm
    c. Nutcracker esophagus
    d. Achalasia

**Answer d.** A dilated proximal esophagus with a classic bird's beak tapering is most consistent with achalasia. You do need to rule out pseudo-achalasia in this patient (a tumor at the GE junction) as well as get manometry to confirm the diagnosis.

319. You suspect this patient has achalasia. You do not see any tumor when you perform EGD. The most important next step in making the diagnosis is:
   a. Manometry
   b. Abd CT
   c. Chest CT
   d. Chest MRI

   **Answer a.** The most important next step in making the diagnosis (after ruling out pseudo-achalasia) is to get manometry.

320. In patients with achalasia, the typical findings on manometry are:
   a. Low LES pressure and absence of peristalsis
   b. Failure of the LES to relax and absence of peristalsis
   c. Normal LES pressure and diffuse simultaneous esophageal contractions
   d. Normal LES pressure and high amplitude peristalsis

   **Answer b.**

   The classic findings of achalasia on manometry are failure of the LES to relax and absence of peristalsis.

   Diffuse esophageal spasm usually presents with a normal LES pressure and diffuse simultaneous esophageal contractions.

   Nutcracker esophagus usually presents with normal LES pressure and high amplitude peristalsis.

321. Pseudo-achalasia:
   a. Is usually caused by an esophageal or gastric tumor
   b. Refers to burned out achalasia
   c. Refers to a hiatal hernia
   d. Occurs after esophagectomy

137

**Answer a.** Pseudo-achalasia is most commonly caused by an esophageal or gastric malignancy (70% of the time). Benign strictures account for most of the rest.

322. During an attempt at balloon dilatation in a patient with achalasia, a gastroenterologist is not able to perform the dilatation. Post-procedure the patient develops chest pain. CXR shows a left effusion. The gastrograffin study is normal but the thin barium study shows a perforation just proximal to the LES that flows freely into the chest. The most appropriate step in management is:
    a. Chest tube
    b. Conservative management
    c. Left thoracotomy
    d. Median sternotomy

**Answer c.** Because there is a free perforation into the left chest, you need to repair the problem operatively (see below).

In the rare case where the perforation is contained, you can go with conservative management (NPO, IVF's, and serial CXR's).

323. Operative repair for the above patient's injury should consist of:
    a. Myotomy to see the extent of the injury followed by repair
    b. Myotomy to see the extent of the injury, repair, and then short segment myotomy on the opposite side of the esophagus
    c. Esophagectomy
    d. Esophageal stent

**Answer b.** In order to repair the perforation and make the repair last, you need to perform a short segment myotomy on the side opposite the perforation to relieve the obstruction.

Then you need a myotomy on the same side as the lesion to see the extent of the mucosal injury.

Then repair the injury, close the myotomy on the side of the injury, and buttress the repair with either intercostal muscle or pleura.

Trying to perform a repair without a short segment myotomy is likely to fail because you have not relieved the distal obstruction associated with achalasia (the LES).

324. A 65 yo cachetic man with an apical lung cancer presents with swollen face, arms and hands. The best treatment for this patient's condition is:
   a. Chemotherapy
   b. XRT
   c. Resection
   d. Antibiotics

**Answer b.** This patient most likely has Superior Vena Cava (SVC) syndrome due to cancer in-growth into the SVC. Treatment of this requires problem requires XRT.

Resection is possible if just a very small portion of the SVC is involved with the lesion (usually found at the time of thoracotomy). Resection is not indicated if the patient has SVC syndrome.

Invasion of the SVC is considered a T4 tumor.

325. A 65 yo cachetic man with an apical lung cancer presents with ptosis, miosis, and anhydrosis. These symptoms are most likely from:
   a. A paraneoplastic syndrome
   b. Invasion of the brachial plexus
   c. Invasion of the SVC
   d. Invasion of the sympathetic chain at T1

**Answer d.**

Pancoast Tumors (superior sulcus tumors) can present w/ either:
Invasion of the brachial plexus (with ulnar nerve symptoms occurring most commonly) or;

Invasion of the sympathetic chain at T1, which results in ptosis, miosis, and anhydrosis (Horner's syndrome).

— Superior sulcus tumors that invade the sympathetic chain ganglia only or just the lowest nerve root of the brachial plexus can still be resected.

326. A 65 yo man with COPD has lung cancer that you are contemplating resecting. You get pulmonary function tests which show an FEV-1 of 1400 cc. This patient likely:
   a.  Could tolerate either a pneumonectomy or lobectomy
   b.  Could tolerate a lobectomy but not pneumonectomy
   c.  Could tolerate wedge resection but not lobectomy
   d.  Could not tolerate any surgery

**Answer b.** A pneumonectomy would leave this patient with an FEV-1 of about 700 (roughly 50% of the initial 1400). The predicted post-op FEV-1 needs to be $\geq 800$ to give a reasonable chance of not being ventilator dependent. (Note, to be precise, the right lung is 55% and the left lung is 45% of total ventilation)

327. A 65 yo man with COPD has lung cancer that you are contemplating resecting. The cancer is completely obstructing the right mainstem bronchus and you may have to perform a pneumonectomy to remove it. You get pulmonary function tests on the patient which show and FEV-1 of 1400 cc. V/Q scan shows 10% ventilation and 10% perfusion to the right lung. This patient:
   a.  Could tolerate either a pneumonectomy or lobectomy
   b.  Could tolerate a lobectomy but not pneumonectomy

c.  Could tolerate wedge resection but not lobectomy
d.  Could not tolerate any surgery

**Answer a.** Because the right lung only receives 10% of the total perfusion, you are only going to lose 10% of the FEV-1 of 1400, leaving you with an FEV-1 of 1260.

A little confusing, but you use the perfusion portion of the V/Q scan to decide what effect resection will have on lung function (not the ventilation portion).

328. A 35 yo woman has progressive symptoms of myasthenia gravis despite maximal medical therapy (steroids, plasmaphereis, and Tensilon). You order a chest CT but do not see any thymoma or thymic enlargement. The most appropriate management in this patient is:
    a.  Resect thymus anyway
    b.  XRT to thymus
    c.  Continued medical therapy and no thymic resection
    d.  Re-CT in 6 months

**Answer a.** In some patients with myasthenia gravis that is refractory to medical therapy, removal of a normal thymus (or even hypotrophic thymus) can result in improvement of symptoms. Thymectomy is indicated in this patient.

329. Myasthenia gravis affects:
    a.  Beta adrenergic receptors
    b.  Alpha-adrenergic receptors
    c.  Acetylcholine receptors
    d.  Dopamine receptors

**Answer c.** Myasthenia gravis involves the formation of antibodies to acetylcholine receptors which impairs binding of acetylcholine.

141

330. A 55 yo man undergoes a right pneumonectomy for lung cancer. Six days after resection, the patient develops fevers, serosanguinous sputum production, and the air-fluid level in the post-pneumonectomy space is lower on CXR. There is also a new infiltrate in the left lower lobe. The most appropriate next step is:
    a. Bronchoscopy
    b. Chest CT
    c. V/Q scan
    d. Antibiotics

**Answer a.** The combination of serosanguinous sputum production, change in air-fluid level, and a new infiltrate is highly suggestive of a broncho-pleural fistula.

The new infiltrate is formed from aspiration into the remaining lung of the residual fluid in the post-pneumonectomy air space.

Broncho-pulmonary fistulas are more common after pneumonectomy compared to lobectomy.

The best way to diagnose the problem is with bronchoscopy.

331. Bronchoscopy in the above patient reveals a bronchopleural fistula. The most appropriate next step in management is:
    a. Antibiotics
    b. Chest tube
    c. Thoracotomy, cover the stump with a muscle flap
    d. nothing

**Answer c.** The best treatment for a bronchopleural fistula is washout of the chest, attempt closure of the stump itself, placement of muscle flap over the bronchus, appropriate drainage, and antibiotics.

332. A 57 yo man has a 3 cm mass in the RLL on chest CT. Biopsy of the mass shows adenocarcinoma. You perform a mediastinoscopy and a right paratracheal lymph node is positive for cancer. The most appropriate next step is:
   a. Perform right lower lobe resection only
   b. Perform right lower lobe resection and mediastinal lymph node dissection
   c. Perform pneumonectomy and mediastinal lymph node dissection
   d. Chemo-XRT

   **Answer d**. Positive paratracheal nodes identified on mediastinoscopy are considered N2 disease and the patient is unresectable. Chemo-XRT is the answer.

   Some protocols would have the patient undergo chemo-XRT and if the patient had a great response, resection of the primary tumor along with mediastinal lymph node dissection.

## Cardiac

333. All of the following are true of congenital heart disease except:
   a. Tetralogy of Fallot is the most common cyanotic congenital heart disease
   b. Ventricular septal defect is the most common congenital heart defect
   c. Tet spells are often self treated by squatting
   d. Trans-esophageal Echo is better than a swan ganz catheter at assessing pulmonary vascular resistance

   **Answer d.** ECHO cannot assess pulmonary vascular resistance (cannot figure out the pulmonary artery and wedge pressure which is required for the calculation. PVR = [(PA pressure – wedge) /cardiac output] x 80

   VSD is the most common congenital heart defect.

   Tetralogy of Fallot is the most common cyanotic congenital heart defect. Squatting improves pulmonary blood flow during a tet spell by increasing systemic vascular resistance, forcing a left to right shunt at the level of the VSD.

334. All of the following are true of the internal mammary artery except:
   a. Is a branch of the subclavian artery
   b. It divides into the musculophrenic and superior epigastric
   c. Has branches to the intercostal arteries
   d. Is a branch of the thoracoacromial artery

   **Answer d.** The internal mammary is a branch of the subclavian artery.

335. The most important determinant of oxygen consumption is:
   a. Heart rate
   b. Wall tension

144

c.   Stroke volume
d.   Preload


**Answer b.** Although both heart rate and wall tension are the factors involved in myocardial oxygen consumption, wall tension is the primary determinant.


336. A 57 yo man with a myocardial infarction 7 days ago suddenly has a new murmur and hypotension requiring volume and pressors. The most appropriate next step in diagnosis is:
   a.   Swan ganz catheter
   b.   ECHO
   c.   Pericardial window
   d.   Chest CT


**Answer b.** A new murmur and hypotension 7 days after a myocardial infarction is worrisome for either acute mitral valve insufficiency (either due to a ruptured chordae or papillary muscle) or due to a post-infarct VSD. ECHO will figure it out.


337. Which of the following risk factors is highest for mortality after CABG surgery?
   a.   Older age
   b.   History of congestive heart failure
   c.   Prior myocardial infarction
   d.   Pre-operative cardiogenic shock


**Answer d.** The biggest risk factor for mortality after CABG is pre-operative cardiogenic shock.

*   Thus, patients with shock after an MI are best served with PTCA, an IABP, and medical therapy rather than a CABG early on.

338. The most common disease process causing ascending aortic aneurysms is:
   a.  Trauma
   b.  Atherosclerosis
   c.  Cystic medial necrosis
   d.  Infection

**Answer c.** Cystic medial necrosis (usually associated with Marfan's) is the most common etiology of ascending aortic aneurysms.

339. The most common disease process causing descending aortic aneurysms is:
   a.  Trauma
   b.  Atherosclerosis
   c.  Cystic medial necrosis
   d.  Infection

**Answer b.** The most common disease process causing descending aortic aneurysms is atherosclerosis.

340. The patency rate of an internal mammary artery to the left anterior descending artery and saphenous vein graft to any other coronary artery are:
   a.  IMA – 90% 20 year patency, SVG – 80% 5 year patency
   b.  SVG – 90% 20 year patency, IMA – 80% 5 year patency
   c.  IMA – 50% 20 year patency, SVG – 40% 5 year patency
   d.  SVG – 50% 20 year patency, IMA – 40% 5 year patency

**Answer a.** An internal mammary artery graft to the left anterior descending artery has a patency of about 90% at 20 years. Saphenous vein grafts have patency rates of 80% at 5 years.

146

## Vascular

341. All of the following are true of popliteal artery aneurysms except:
    a. The most common complication is rupture
    b. Thrombosis can occur
    c. They are often bilateral
    d. Emboli is the most common complication

    **Answer a.** Aneurysms below the inguinal ligament rarely rupture. The most common complication is embolization, followed by thrombosis.

342. Which organ does not contain lymphatics:
    a. Lung
    b. Liver
    c. Spleen
    d. Muscle

    **Answer d.** Organs that do not contain lymphatics are the brain, tendons, muscle, bone, cartilage, and cornea.

343. Patients who have popliteal artery aneurysms should be screened for:
    a. Thoracic outlet syndrome
    b. Abdominal aneurysms
    c. Atherosclerotic disease
    d. Syphilis

    **Answer b.** Patients with a popliteal artery aneurysm are at high risk for bilateral popliteal artery aneurysms (50%), abdominal aortic aneurysms, and other aneurysms.

344. The most common cause of abdominal aortic aneurysms is:

147

a. Trauma
b. Atherosclerosis
c. Cystic medial necrosis
d. Infection

**Answer b.** The most common etiology of abdominal aortic aneurysms is atherosclerosis.

345. A 50 yo man in atrial fibrillation and no history of peripheral vascular disease develops a cold painful right leg after forgetting to take his coumadin. Pulses on the left side are normal. The most appropriate next step in management is:
a. Thrombolytics
b. Embolectomy
c. Arterial bypass
d. Nothing

**Answer b.** Given the above history, embolus is the most likely cause of the cold, painful right leg. Embolectomy is the treatment of choice.

346. Four hours after successful embolectomy, the above patient develops a swollen painful right leg that feels tight to exam. He has pain with passive motion of the leg. The most appropriate next step in management is:
a. Fasciotomy
b. Arterial bypass
c. Lasix
d. Heparin

**Answer a.** Reperfusion injury resulting in compartment syndrome can occur after restoration of blood flow if the occlusion time has been more than 4-6 hours.

Prophylactic fasciotomies should be considered in these patients.

Compartment syndrome is a clinical diagnosis – if you think it is present, go ahead with fasciotomy.

A compartment pressure > 20 mmHg is suggestive of compartment syndrome.

347. Electrolyte abnormalities in the above scenario include:
    a. hyponatremia
    b. hypercalcemia
    c. hypermagnesemia
    d. hyperkalemia

    **Answer d.** Hyperkalemia from myonecrosis can occur in patients with compartment syndrome.

348. A 50 yo man in normal sinus rhythm with a history of peripheral vascular disease including a previous femoral to popliteal bypass on the right side develops a cool and mildly painful right leg. The leg does not look threatened. Pulses on the left side are somewhat diminished but this appears to be baseline. The most appropriate next step in management is:
    a. Thrombolytics
    b. Embolectomy
    c. Arterial bypass
    d. Nothing

    **Answer a.** This patient most likely has thrombosis of the right extremity. Because the leg is not threatened, thrombolytics are probably the best option for this patient.

    Given the above, just operating on the patient and performing a thrombectomy is also reasonable and the treatment of choice if the leg is threatened.

149

349. A 60 yo man develops TIA's and has a carotid ultrasound that shows an 80% stenosis. The most appropriate next step in management is:
   a. Plavix
   b. ASA
   c. Carotid endarterectomy
   d. Nothing

   **Answer c.** Patients with symptoms from carotid disease and a stenosis ≥ 60% should have CEA. Asymptomatic patients and stenosis ≥ 70% should have CEA. Some groups prefer to perform angiogram before CEA.

350. Two hours after CEA, the above patient develops a neurologic deficit while in the post-anesthesia care unit. The most appropriate next step in management is:
   a. Head CT
   b. Head MRI
   c. Angiography
   d. Re-exploration

   **Answer d.** Patients with an acute event post-op following a CEA should be taken back to the operating room for re-exploration.

   You will need to see if a flap formed, thrombosis occurred at the suture line, hematoma caused compression of the carotid, or if some other reason caused the neurological event.

351. The most commonly injured nerve with CEA is:
   a. vagus
   b. hypoglossal
   c. lingual
   d. glossopharyngeal

150

**Answer a.** The most commonly injured nerve is the vagus nerve. Because the recurrent laryngeal nerve has not branched off the vagus nerve yet at this level, injury to the vagus nerve in the neck places the patient at risk for hoarseness.

352. Four days after AAA repair, your patient develops bloody diarrhea and some abdominal distension. The most appropriate next step in management is:
    a. Flagyl
    b. Re-exploration
    c. Protamine
    d. Sigmoidoscopy

**Answer d.** A patient who has bloody diarrhea (or any diarrhea this early after a AAA repair) needs to be evaluated for ischemic colitis. Ischemic colitis usually occurs from ligation of the inferior mesenteric artery.

The best method to evaluate for ischemic colitis is to perform sigmoidoscopy.

Remember to go past the rectum and into the sigmoid and descending colon to the splenic flexure to evaluate for injury (preservation of the rectum occurs because the inferior and middle rectal arteries come off the internal iliac artery and not the inferior mesenteric artery).

353. Sigmoidoscopy in the above patient reveals a black upper rectum and sigmoid colon. The most appropriate next step in management is:
    a. Flagyl
    b. Resection, colostomy, and Hartman's Pouch
    c. Rectal stent
    d. Nothing

**Answer b.** This patient has a necrotic upper rectum and sigmoid colon. This patient needs resection of the area.

354. The above complication occurs from injury to:
   a. The right colic artery
   b. The inferior mesenteric artery
   c. The middle colic artery
   d. The inferior rectal artery

   **Answer b.** This complication occurs from injury to (or
   ligation of) the inferior mesenteric artery.

355. A 55 yo woman in the medical intensive care unit has a PMHx
   significant for atrial fibrillation and peripheral vascular disease.
   She has recently developed pneumonia and has required
   intubation. Over the past 7 days, they have been holding her anti-
   coagulation. They have also started her on levophed and
   vasopressin for hypotension presumed to be from sepsis. They
   have called you because her abdomen has become progressively
   more distended and she now has guaiac positive stools (but not
   gross melana). She is tender but does not have gross peritoneal
   signs. Her lactic acid is 7 and her white count is 20. Her blood
   pressure is 100/60 and heart rate is 90. She is currently on broad
   spectrum antibiotics. The next appropriate step in management of
   this patient is:
   a. Laparotomy
   b. Peritoneal tap
   c. CT scan
   d. Angiogram

   **Answer d.** This patient may have mesenteric ischemia.
   There are a variety of options for this patient in terms of
   management. She is in the middle ground.

   Going to CT scan or just performing a laparotomy are not
   totally unreasonable, but going to angiogram 1<sup>st</sup> when you are
   not sure what is going on is probably the most logical next
   step.

   If the angiogram shows just constricted vessels from all of the
   pressors agents she is on (non-occlusive mesenteric ischemia
   – NOMI), then you can start directed intra-arterial infusion of

papavarine or nitroglycerin directly into the culprit vessel, improving blood flow to that portion of the intestine. The patient will need to be explored if her clinical situation does not improve or if she gets peritoneal signs.

If this turns out to be an embolus, take the patient to the OR for open embolectomy (TPA for an embolus generally does not work).

If this turns out to be a thrombosis, angio allows the opportunity of thrombolysis with TPA and also gives you a road map of where to perform your bypasses if you decide to go with operative therapy.

356. The angiogram you ordered in the above patient shows a meniscus sign 5 cm down from the take-off of the superior mesenteric artery. The jejunal branches proximal to this are normal. This patient most likely has:
    a. Non-occlusive mesenteric ischemia
    b. SMA thrombosis
    c. SMA embolus
    d. Venous thrombosis

**Answer c.** A meniscus sign and sparing of the proximal jejunal branches is most consistent with SMA embolus.

357. Management of the above patient requires:
    a. Continued ICU management
    b. Direct papavarine injection
    c. SMA embolectomy, resection of necrotic bowel, 2$^{nd}$ look tomorrow
    d. SMA thrombectomy, SMA bypass, resection of necrotic bowel, 2$^{nd}$ look tomorrow

**Answer c.** This patient should go to the OR for embolectomy, resection of necrotic bowel, and a 2$^{nd}$ look procedure the next day.

358. Instead of the above finding, the angiogram shows proximal narrowing right at the take-off of the SMA with involvement of the proximal jejunal vessels. The celiac artery is also occluded. This is most consistent with:
   a. Non-occlusive mesenteric ischemia
   b. SMA thrombosis
   c. SMA embolus
   d. Venous thrombosis

   **Answer b.** Two vessel disease and narrowing right at the takeoff of the SMA is most consistent with SMA thrombosis.

359. Management of superior mesenteric artery thrombosis in a patient with gross peritoneal signs is:
   a. Continued ICU management
   b. Direct papavarine injection
   c. SMA embolectomy, resection of necrotic bowel, $2^{nd}$ look tomorrow
   d. SMA thrombectomy, SMA bypass, resection of necrotic bowel, $2^{nd}$ look tomorrow

   **Answer d.** The above patient should have SMA thrombectomy, resection of necrotic bowel, SMA bypass, and a $2^{nd}$ look the next day.

   One could also consider catheter directed thrombolytic therapy in this patient as long if there were no peritoneal signs or any gross melana.

## Gastrointestinal Hormones

360. Parietal cells of the stomach secrete:
   a. HCL and intrinsic factor
   b. Pepsinogen
   c. Secretin
   d. Cholecystokinin

   **Answer a.** The parietal cells secrete HCL and intrinsic factor (which binds B-12 and eventually gets reabsorbed primarily in the terminal ileum).

361. Chief cells of the stomach secrete:
   a. HCL and intrinsic factor
   b. Pepsinogen
   c. Secretin
   d. Cholecystokinin

   **Answer b.** Chief cells primarily secrete pepsinogen. This is the first enzyme to start protein digestion after eating.

   Salivary amylase is the first enzyme to start carbohydrate digestion after eating.

   Amylase is the only enzyme secreted by the pancrease in active form.

362. Intrinsic factor binds:
   a. Fe
   b. Cu
   c. B-12
   d. B-6

   **Answer c.** Intrinsic factor binds B-12.

363. Omeprazole works by:
   a. Inhibiting the parietal cell H/K ATPase
   b. Blocking histamine receptor
   c. Blocking acetylcholine receptors
   d. Blocking TSH receptors

**Answer a.** Omeprazole works by inhibiting the parietal cell H/K ATPase.

364. Zantac works by:
   a. Inhibiting the parietal cell H/K ATPase
   b. Blocking histamine receptors
   c. Blocking acetylcholine receptors
   d. Blocking TSH receptors

**Answer b.** Zantac works by inhibiting the histamine receptor.

365. Most common problem following vagotomy and pyloroplasty is:
   a. Diarrhea
   b. Dumping syndrome
   c. Gallstones
   d. Alkaline reflux gastritis

**Answer a.** Diarrhea is the most common problem following vagotomy.

Dumping syndrome

From rapid entering of carbohydrates into small bowel

90% resolve medically

2 parts

156

1. Hyperosmotic load in bowel causes fluid shift
   (hypotension, can also get diarrhea, dizziness)
2. Insulin release with hypoglycemia (2nd phase
   rarely occurs)

Treatment:
    Small meals, high protein, low-fat, low-carbohydrate
    Avoid liquids with a meal
    Avoid lying down after a meal
    Octreotide usually effective (take before meals)

Surgical options (rarely necessary):
    Roux-en-Y gastrojejunostomy (from BI or BII)
    Increase gastric reservoir (jejunal pouch)
    Increase emptying time (reversed jejunal loop)

Alkaline reflux gastritis

    Postprandial epigastric pain
    Nausea and vomiting - Pain not relieved with vomiting
    Diagnosis: EGD - bile reflux in stomach, gastritis on Bx
    Treatment: PPI, cholestyramine, metoclopramide
    Surgical option:
        Roux-en-Y gastrojejunostomy with afferent limb 60
        cm distal to original gastrojejunostomy
        (conversion from BI or BII)

Post-vagotomy diarrhea

    From sustained postprandial organized MMC's
    Results in non-conjugated bile salts into colon
    Treatment: cholestyramine, octreotide
    Surgical options (rarely necessary): reversed interposition
        jejunal graft

366. Most water is absorbed in the:
    a.   Stomach
    b.   Duodenum
    c.   Jejunum

157

d.  Colon


**Answer c.**  90% of all water is absorbed in the proximal jejunum.

## Esophagus

367. The UES pressure at rest and during the early part of the swallow are approximately:
   a.   70 mmHg and 15 mmHg
   b.   15 mmHg and 70 mmHg
   c.   15 mmHg and 0 mmHg
   d.   0 mmHg and 15 mmHg

**Answer a.** The upper esophageal sphincter (cricopharyngeous muscle) pressures at rest and during the early part of a swallow are approximately 70 mmHg and 15 mmHg respectively.

Patients with Zenker's Diverticula typically have elevated UES pressures with swallowing because the cricopharyngeous muscle fails to relax.

368. The LES pressure at rest and during a swallow are approximately:
   a.   70 mmHg and 15 mmHg
   b.   15 mmHg and 70 mmHg
   c.   15 mmHg and 0 mmHg
   d.   0 mmHg and 15 mmHg

**Answer c.** The approximate LES pressure at rest is 15 mmHg and during a swallow it is 0 mmHg.

Patients with GERD typically have lower LES pressures at rest.

369. The most important step in treatment of a patient with a Zenker's diverticulum is:
   a.   Resection of the diverticulum
   b.   Division of the superior laryngeal constrictor muscles
   c.   Esophagectomy
   d.   Division of the cricopharyngeous muscle

159

**Answer d.** The most important step in treatment of a Zenker's diverticulum is performing a cricopharyngomyotomy.

The anatomic problem with a Zenker's diverticulum is failure of the UES to relax with swallowing.

The diverticulum is usually resected but in some situations when the diverticulum would be too hard to remove, it can be suspended upward such that it drains into the esophagus.

370. The most sensitive test for gastro-esophageal reflux disease is:
   a.  Barium swallow
   b.  Endoscopic biopsy
   c.  Manometry
   d.  24 pH study

**Answer d.** The most sensitive test for GERD is the 24 hour pH study.

371. Indications for surgical repair of a hiatal hernia in a symptomatic patient includes all of the following except:
   a.  Patient desires not to take pills to control reflux for a prolonged period
   b.  Regurgitation and aspiration not controlled with medical therapy
   c.  Persistent symptoms despite medical therapy
   d.  Low grade Barrett's Esophagus

**Answer d.** Barrett's is not an indication for hiatal hernia repair although the patient should be placed on a proton pump inhibitor and have their esophagus evaluated for dysplasia and cancer on a regular basis.

The other items listed are indications for hiatal hernia repair.

372. A 50 yo man with long standing reflux undergoes upper
     endoscopy which reveals high grade dysplasia. The most
     appropriate therapy in this patient is:
     a. Esophagectomy
     b. Photodynamic therapy
     c. Proton pump inhibitor
     d. Metochlopromide

     **Answer a.** High grade dysplasia is an indication for
     esophagectomy. Up to 20% of patients with high grade
     dysplasia actually have esophageal CA somewhere in the
     Barrett's portion of the esophagus.

373. Barrett's esophagus refers to:
     a. The change in esophageal mucosa from columnar to
        squamous
     b. The change in esophageal mucosa to transitional
        epithelium
     c. Keratinization of the esophageal mucosa
     d. Change in esophageal mucosa from squamous to
        columnar epithelium

     **Answer d.** Barrett's refers to the change in esophageal
     epithelium from squamous to columnar.

374. The relative risk of esophageal cancer patients with Barrett's
     esophagus is:
     a. 5
     b. 10
     c. 50
     d. 100

     **Answer c.** The presence of Barrett's increases the relative
     risk of esophageal CA to 50.

375. Treatment of esophageal leiomyoma involves:
   a. Enucleation
   b. Esophagectomy
   c. XRT
   d. Chemotherapy

**Answer a.** Treatment of esophageal leiomyoma is enucleation through a thoracotomy.

These lesions are typically confined to the muscularis propria and do not have a mucosal component.

Notably, you do not want to try and biopsy leiomyomas with an EGD because you can create scar tissue around the tumor which will make taking the leiomyoma out difficult and will increase the likelihood of disrupting the mucosa.

376. A 65 yo man undergoes an Ivor Lewis esophagectomy. On post-op day # 6, he develops a fever of 103 and a white blood cell count of 18. You start intravenous fluids and send off cultures. The most appropriate next step in management is:
   a. Chest CT
   b. Abdominal CT
   c. Gastrograffin followed by thin barium swallow
   d. Chest MRI

**Answer c.** One of the most feared complications following esophagectomy is the development of an esophageal leak. This is usually manifested by fevers and an elevated white blood cell count. Severe leaks can result in tachycardia and hypotension.

The diagnostic study of choice to see whether or not the patient has a leak is a gastrograffin followed by thin barium swallow.

377. The barium study in the above patient shows a non-contained contrast leak at the level of the anastomosis. The most appropriate next step in management is:
    a.   Chest tube
    b.   Re-exploration
    c.   Esophageal stent
    d.   Upper endoscopy

**Answer b.** This patient needs re-exploration to find the source of the leak.

378. You re-explore the above patient and find that the gastric conduit looks viable but there is a pinhole leak on the top of your suture line. The surrounding tissue looks viable. The most appropriate next step in management is:
    a.   Take conduit down and perform esophagostomy
    b.   Repair the defect and then place an intercostal muscle flap
    c.   Lay a drain over the hole only
    d.   Place an esophageal stent

**Answer b.** Finding just a tiny hole in the esophagus can be repaired although you should re-enforce the repair with a pleural, pericardial fat, or intercostal muscle flap to cover the area. You should also place drains.

Keep the patient NPO for a week, repeat the swallow after that. J-tube feeds until the swallow.

Although esophagostomy for diversion away from the repair could be considered for the above patient, it is probably a little too aggressive.

379. Instead of finding a tiny hole in the above patient, you find that the stomach has a large area of necrosis. The most appropriate next step in management is:
    a.   Take conduit down and perform esophagostomy

b.  Repair the defect and then place an intercostal muscle flap
c.  Lay a drain over the hole
d.  Place an esophageal stent

**Answer a.** In this scenario, you would need to takedown the anastomosis, resect the necrotic portion of stomach, place drains, and perform an esophagostomy. Wait 3 months before attempting to re-connect the patient (likely with a colonic interposition).

## Stomach

380. A 50 yo man presents with epigastric pain unrelieved with proton pump inhibitors. You perform an upper endoscopy and a mass is found in the stomach mucosa *only*. You biopsy it and it comes back lympho-proliferative tissue. The next appropriate therapy is:
    a. Total gastrectomy
    b. Partial gastrectomy
    c. Chemo-XRT therapy
    d. Triple therapy for H pylori

    **Answer d.** Mucosa associated lymphoproliferative tissue is related to H pylori infection and is considered a precursor to lymphoma.

    Initial treatment of MALT is triple therapy (amoxicillin, tetracycline, proton pump inhibitor) for H pylori. You can also substitute flagyl for tetracycline.

381. You treat the above patient for 3 months with proton pump inhibitors, amoxicillin, and tetracycline however the lesion persists on repeat biopsy. The next appropriate therapy is:
    a. Total gastrectomy
    b. Partial gastrectomy
    c. Chemo-XRT therapy
    d. Triple therapy for H pylori for another 3 months

    **Answer c.** If the above therapy fails, the patient should get chemo-XRT.

382. A 50 yo man presents with epigastric pain unrelieved with proton pump inhibitors. You perform an upper endoscopy and a mass is found in the stomach. You biopsy it and it comes back as a malignant stromal tumor (gastro-intestinal stromal tumor). The patient undergoes resection but post-op pathology shows metastases in the liver. The next appropriate therapy is:
    a. Radiation therapy

165

b. 5 fluorouracil and cisplatnin
c. Gleevec
d. Do nothing

**Answer c.** Gleevec, a tyrosine kinase inhibitor, has been found to be extremely effective for metastatic gastro-intestinal stromal tumors.

383. The left gastric artery:
a. Is a branch off the celiac axis
b. Is a branch of the right gastric artery
c. Is a branch of the common hepatic artery
d. Is a branch of the splenic artery

**Answer a.** The left gastric artery is a branch off the celiac axis.

384. A patient with a history of pancreatitis develops severe bleeding from gastric varices. You do not see any esophageal varices on EGD. The best treatment for this patient is:
a. Splenectomy
b. TIPS procedure
c. Spleno-renal shunt
d. Porto-caval shunt

**Answer a.** Gastric varices without esophageal varices are most likely from a thrombosed splenic vein related to pancreatitis and not cirrhosis. Less than 2-3% of patients with cirrhosis get gastric varices without esophageal varices.

Treatment in this patient is splenectomy.

385. A 50 yo man presents with epigastric pain unrelieved with proton pump inhibitors. You perform an upper endoscopy and a mass is

found in the stomach. You biopsy it and it comes back lymphoma. Abdominal CT scan shows that the mass is full thickness and ¾ of the stomach is involved. The most appropriate therapy in this patient is:

    a.  Total gastrectomy
    b.  Partial gastrectomy
    c.  Chemo-XRT
    d.  Triple therapy for H pylori


**Answer c.** Treatment for gastric lymphoma is chemo-XRT. Surgery is indicated only for complications of the disease (bleeding, perforation, obstruction) or possibly for stage I disease limited to the mucosa.

## Liver

386. A 40 yo woman from Greece presents to the emergency room with abdominal pain. Abdominal CT scan shows a calcified cyst in the liver. She has a positive Casoni skin test sent by fax from Greece. The most appropriate next step is:
    a. Percutaneous drainage
    b. Albendazole
    c. Liver resection
    d. Flagyl

    **Answer b.** You should never perform percutaneous drainage in patients with echinococcal cysts as spillage of the cyst can cause a severe anaphylactic reaction.

    Treatment consists of pre-op albendazole flowed by resection of the cyst.

387. A schistosomiasis abscess is best treated with:
    a. Percutaneous drainage and antibiotics
    b. Flagyl
    c. Levofloxacin
    d. Praziquantel

    **Answer d.** The treatment of a schistosomiasis liver abscess is Praziquantel. These cysts need percutaneous drainage only for super-infection. Surgery is only for complications such as bleeding.

    These patients can also get esophageal varices.

388. An amoebic abscess is best treated with:
    a. Percutaneous drainage and antibiotics
    b. Flagyl
    c. Levofloxacin
    d. Praziquantel

**Answer b.** An amoebic abscess is best treated with flagyl. Percutaneous drainage is needed only for super-infection. Surgery is needed only for complications such as bleeding.

389. An pyogenic abscess is best treated with:
     a. Percutaneous drainage and antibiotics
     b. Flagyl
     c. Levofloxacin
     d. Praziquantel

**Answer a.** A pyogenic abscess is best treated with broad spectrum antibiotics and percutaneous drainage. GNR's are the most common organism in these cysts. You should also cover for anaerobes.

Liver abscesses can arise weeks after an episode of diverticulitis or appendicitis or other intra-abdominal infectious process.

390. A 25 yo woman develops jaundice and ascites 2 weeks after child-birth. This is most likely related to:
     a. Retained placenta
     b. Hepatocellular carcinoma
     c. Biliary cystadenocarcinoma
     d. Hepatic vein thrombosis

**Answer d.** Post-partum hepatic vein thrombosis (Post-partum Budd Chiari Syndrome) is rare and related to the relative hypercoaguable state that occurs following pregnancy. Patients with hypercoaguable syndromes seem more susceptible to the problem.

The best test for post-partum hepatic vein thrombosis is a mesenteric angiogram with venous phase contrast. MRI

169

would also be a useful test but it is not as sensitive as an angiogram.

391. A 40 yo woman on <u>no</u> medications and without any past medical problems presents with intermittent abdominal discomfort. She undergoes a contrasted abdominal CT scan which shows a 4 cm hypervascular liver lesion. Sulfur colloid scan shows no uptake. AFP is normal. There is no peripheral to central enhancement on the contrasted CT scan. The most appropriate next step is:
   a.   Resection
   b.   Follow the lesion
   c.   Steroids
   d.   Liver biopsy

   **Answer a.** A liver mass that is hypervascular, is associated with a normal AFP (likely not hepatocellular carcinoma), has no peripheral to central enhancement (likely not a hemangioma), and no uptake on sulfur colloid scan (likely not focal nodular hyperplasia) is most consistent with adenoma.

   Because she is not on any steroids (i.e. oral contraceptive pills), the treatment for the lesion is resection because of the significant risk of rupture and malignant transformation.

392. A 40 yo woman on no medications and without any past medical problems presents with intermittent abdominal pain. She undergoes a contrasted abdominal CT scan which shows a 4 cm hypervascular liver lesion and some necrotic areas within the mass. Sulfur colloid scan shows no uptake. AFP is 500. There is no peripheral to central enhancement on the contrasted CT scan. The most appropriate next step is:
   a.   Resection if the lesion is resectable
   b.   Follow the lesion
   c.   Steroids
   d.   Liver biopsy

**Answer a.** A liver mass that is hypervascular with necrotic areas, is associated with a high AFP, has no peripheral to central enhancement (likely not a hemangioma), and no uptake on sulfur colloid scan (likely not focal nodular hyperplasia) is most consistent with hepatocellular carcinoma.

The treatment of the lesion is resection if the tumor is resectable.

393. A 40 yo woman on no medications or past medical problems presents with intermittent abdominal pain. She undergoes a contrasted abdominal CT scan which shows a 4 cm hypervascular liver lesion. Sulfur colloid scan shows no uptake. AFP is normal. There is obvious peripheral to central enhancement on the contrasted CT scan. The most appropriate next step is:
    a. Resection if the lesion is resectable
    b. Nothing
    c. Steroids
    d. Liver biopsy

**Answer b.** Peripheral to central enhancement is most consistent with hemangioma. No biopsy.

394. A 40 yo woman on no medications or past medical problems presents with intermittent abdominal pain. She undergoes a contrasted abdominal CT scan which shows a 4 cm liver lesion with a definite central stellate scar. Sulfur colloid scan shows increased uptake. AFP is normal. There is no peripheral to central enhancement on the contrasted CT scan. The most appropriate next step is:
    a. Resection if the lesion is resectable
    b. Follow the lesion
    c. Steroids
    d. Liver biopsy

**Answer b.** Because of the central stellate scar and the positive sulfur colloid scan, this lesion is most consistent with focal nodular hyperplasia and does not need resection.

You should follow the lesion to make sure its not getting any bigger. Finding the central stellate scar and having uptake on sulfur colloid scan are not 100% so you should follow the lesion for a while.

395. The most common right hepatic artery variant is:
   a.  Off the inferior mesenteric artery
   b.  Off the left gastric
   c.  Off the splenic artery
   d.  Off the superior mesenteric artery

**Answer d.** The most common variant of the right hepatic artery comes off the superior mesenteric artery. This artery travels in the hepato-duodenal ligament laterally (usually).

396. The most common left hepatic artery variant is:
   a.  Off the superior mesenteric artery
   b.  Off the left gastric
   c.  Off the splenic artery
   d.  Off the inferior mesenteric artery

**Answer b.** The most common left hepatic artery variant comes off the left gastric artery. This artery then travels in the gastro-hepatic ligament.

# Biliary system

397. A 55 yo woman presents to the emergency room with crampy abdominal pain. On plain film of her abdomen, you notice multiple air-fluid levels and distension of her small bowel. Her colon appears decompressed. She also has pneumobilia despite never having surgery before or manipulation of her biliary system. The most appropriate next step is:
    a. Start broad spectrum antibiotics
    b. Exploratory laparotomy
    c. Percutaneous cholecystostomy tube
    d. Endoscopic retrograde cholangiography

    **Answer b.** Pneumobilia (in a patient who has never had manipulation of her biliary system) associated with small bowel obstruction is most consistent with gallstone ileus. The gallbladder in this patient has eroded into the duodenum and a large gallstone is now causing a small bowel obstruction. This patient needs exploration.

398. The primary surgery for patients with gallstone ileus consists of:
    a. Open the ileum and removing the obstruction
    b. Whipple
    c. Cholecystectomy
    d. Hepaticojejunostomy

    **Answer a.** The primary surgery in this patient is to relieve the small bowel obstruction. That involves feeling for the gallstone, opening the ileum, and removing the stone.

    The secondary procedure, if the patient can tolerate it, is cholecystectomy and closure of the hole in the duodenum.

399. A 50 yo woman undergoes routine laparoscopic cholecystectomy and gallbladder adenocarcinoma is found extending into the muscular layer. The next appropriate step in management is:

    a.   Wedge resection of segment 1
    b.   Wedge resection of segment 3
    c.   Wedge resection of segment 5
    d.   Wedge resection of segment 7

**Answer c.** Gallbladder adenocarcinoma confined to the mucosa can be treated with just cholecystectomy.

If it invades the muscularis, you need wedge resection of segments 4 and 5 (some would just perform segmentectomies of those areas to avoid bleeding) and stripping of the lymph nodes along the portal triad.

400. During a very difficult laparoscopic cholecystectomy, you perform an intra-op cholangiogram and notice good distal filling of the common bile duct, but no filling of the proximal hepatic duct despite changes in patient position. The most appropriate next step is:
    a.   Open
    b.   Place Jackson Pratt drains
    c.   Place a T-tube
    d.   Broad spectrum antibiotics

**Answer a.** You should open and find out what the problem is. Lack of filling in the proximal hepatic duct is worrisome for stricture from a clip across the hepatic duct (which was mistaken for the cystic duct).

401. You explore the above patient and there are 2 clips on the proximal hepatic duct, a divided hepatic duct, and one clip on the distal hepatic duct. The most appropriate next step is:
    a.   Whipple
    b.   End to end anastomosis with absorbable suture
    c.   Hepatico-jejunostomy
    d.   Choledocho-jejunostomy

**Answer c.** The most appropriate step in this patient is to perform a hepatico-jejunostomy. End to end hepatic duct anastomosis usually results in stricture at the anastomosis with these types of injuries so it is not indicated.

Choledocho-jejunostomy would be indicated if the transection occurred at the level of the common bile duct.

402. A 30 yo woman presents to your office 7 days after a laparoscopic cholecystectomy and complains of moderate abdominal pain in the right upper quadrant and nausea. The most appropriate next step is:
   a. RUQ ultrasound
   b. Change pain medications
   c. ERCP
   d. Broad spectrum antibiotics

   **Answer a.** Pain and nausea after laparoscopic cholecystectomy are unusual. Work-up of the problem would start with sending off LFT's and a CBC along with getting an ultrasound of the RUQ.

   One could also consider CT scan but U/S is a more sensitive test.

403. Ultrasound in the above woman reveals a 8 x 8 cm fluid collection in the gall bladder fossa. The most appropriate next step is:
   a. Broad spectrum antibiotics
   b. Re-exploration
   c. ERCP
   d. Percutaneous drainage

   **Answer d.** Given the patient's symptoms and size of the fluid collection, the fluid collection should undergo percutaneous drainage.

175

404. You place a drain in the above patient and it reveals bile fluid. The most appropriate next step in this patient's management is:
   a.  ERCP
   b.  Exploratory laparotomy
   c.  Abdominal CT scan
   d.  Broad spectrum antibiotics

**Answer a.** Bile fluid is worrisome for an injury to the biliary system. This patient should undergo ERCP.

405. ERCP on the above patient shows free extravasation of contrast from the cystic duct remnant. The most appropriate next step is:
   a.  Exploratory laparotomy
   b.  Broad spectrum antibiotics
   c.  PTC tube
   d.  ERCP, sphincterotomy, and stent

**Answer d.** Most likely, the clip fell off the cystic duct remnant and is causing the leakage of bile into the abdomen.

This problem is effectively treated 95+ % of the time with ERCP, sphincterotomy, and a temporary stent.

Eventually, the cystic duct remnant will scar down.

A Duct of Luschka leak can also be treated this way.

More serious injuries would likely require re-operation in 6-8 weeks (along with percutaneous drainage until surgery).

406. A 60 yo woman with no past medical problems presents to the emergency room with jaundice, right upper quadrant pain, and fever. Her blood pressure is 80/40 and her heart rate is 135. The most appropriate next step is:
   a.  Emergent cholecystectomy
   b.  Emergent ERCP
   c.  Emergent PTC placement

d.  Volume resuscitation and IV antibiotics

**Answer d.** This patient needs fluid resuscitation and antibiotics started before any diagnostic studies are performed. From the clinical scenario presented, this patient most likely has cholangitis.

407. The above patient now has a blood pressure of 110/60 and a HR of 100 after appropriate therapy. You obtain an ultrasound while giving her IVF's which shows a dilated common bile duct. The most appropriate next step is:
   a.  Emergent cholecystectomy
   b.  Emergent ERCP
   c.  Emergent PTC placement
   d.  Hepatico-jejunostomy

**Answer b.** The most effective treatment for cholangitis is decompression of the biliary system. This is most easily done with ERCP and sphincterotomy, which not only can decompress the biliary system but can also remove or treat any obstructive lesion (stone most commonly).

408. The gastroenterologist is not able to cannulate the Ampulla of Vater in the above patient. The most appropriate next step is:
   a.  Emergent cholecystectomy
   b.  Emergent PTC placement
   c.  Hepatico-jejunostomy
   d.  T-tube placement

**Answer b.** The next step if ERCP is not effective is to place a PTC (percutaneous trans-hepatic cholangiography) tube to decompress the biliary system.

409. The radiologist is not able to place a PTC tube in the above patient. The most appropriate next step is:
    a. Emergent cholecystectomy
    b. Emergent choledocho-jejunostomy
    c. Emergent Hepatico-jejunostomy
    d. T-tube placement

**Answer d.** The next step in the pathway if the PTC tube cannot be placed is to go to the OR and place a T-tube for decompression.

410. The most common organism involved in cholangitis is:
    a. Staph aureus
    b. Streptococcus
    c. Bacteriodies fragilis
    d. E. coli

**Answer d.** The most common organism involved in cholangitis is E. coli.

411. The most common cause of cholangitis is:
    a. Gallstones
    b. Malignancy
    c. Benign biliary strictures
    d. Iatrogenic injury to the biliary system

**Answer a.** The most common cause of cholangitis is gallstones.

412. A 35 yo woman undergoing routine laparoscopic bilateral tubal ligation develops severe hypotension, tachycardia, and drop in her end-tidal $CO_2$. The anesthesiologist states the patient still has bilateral breath sounds. The most likely diagnosis is:
    a. A disconnection between the patient and the ventilator

b.   The patient has developed atelectasis
c.   Myocardial infarction
d.   CO2 embolus

**Answer d.** End tidal CO2 specifically reflects the exchange of CO2 from blood to the alveolus. A gradual rise in ETCO2 usually reflects impaired exchange from lung collapse or atelectasis.

A sudden drop in ETCO2 can be from something simple like disconnection from the ventilator or something more serious such as an embolus. The abrupt drop in ETCO2 following an embolus is from the interruption of CO2 exchange at the alveolar level.

Because of the hypotension associated with a drop in ETCO2 in the above patient, the most likely diagnosis is CO2 embolus.

413. Treatment of the above problem involves removing the abdominal insufflation and:
a.   Emergent TPA therapy
b.   Coronary catheterization
c.   Bilateral chest tubes
d.   Trendelenburg, left side down, and 100% oxygen

**Answer d.** Treatment of CO2 embolus involves placing the patients head down and the patient on the left side (to prevent any more propagation of CO2 into the lungs)

100% oxygen is given which is absorbed faster than CO2 (the oxygen will come to equilibrium with the CO2 in the embolus and will be reabsorbed faster than the CO2) and will also help oxygenate the patient.

If CPR is needed, it should progress for a prolonged period of time to allow the embolus to be re-absorbed.

179

You should also increase minute ventilation (respiratory rate and tidal volumes) to remove CO2 faster.

414. A 50 yo woman undergoing routine laparoscopic tubal ligation has a sudden drop in her end-tidal CO2. The anesthesiologist states he cannot hear any breath sounds. Her blood pressure is 120/60 and her HR is 70. The most likely diagnosis is:
    a. A disconnection between the patient and the ventilator
    b. The patient has developed atelectasis
    c. Myocardial infarction
    d. CO2 embolus

    **Answer a.** Because this patient is totally stable, the most likely cause of the decreased ETCO2 is disconnection from the ventilator.

415. A 50 yo woman undergoing routine laparoscopic bilateral tubal ligation has a sudden rise in end-tidal CO2. The anesthesiologist states that the patient's breath sounds are present but are decreased in both the bases. Her blood pressure is 120/60 and her HR is 70. The most likely diagnosis is:
    a. A disconnection between the patient and the ventilator
    b. The patient has developed atelectasis
    c. Myocardial infarction
    d. CO2 embolus

    **Answer b.** The most likely cause of the rise in ETCO2 is atelectasis. The patient needs larger tidal volumes most likely.

416. Each of the following is an action of cholecystokinin except:
    a. gallbladder contraction
    b. pancreatic enzyme release
    c. relaxation of the sphincter of Oddi
    d. decreased intestinal motility

180

**Answer d.** CCK causes gallbladder contraction, pancreatic enzyme release, relaxation of the sphincter of Oddi and some increase in intestinal motility.

417. Each of the following is an action of secretin in normal patients except:
   a. Increased bile flow
   b. Inhibits HCL release in the stomach
   c. Increased pancreatic HCO3- release
   d. Increases gastrin release

**Answer d.** Secretin causes increased bile flow, increased pancreatic HCO3- release, and inhibition of HCL and gastrin release from the stomach in normal patients.

Notably, gastrin will go up with secretin injection in patients with gastrinoma.

## Pancreas

418. A 56 yo woman presents to the emergency room with severe abdominal pain. She has no other PMHx. She occasionally drinks. You get routine labs which are significant for an amylase of 24,000 and lipase of 7000. AXR's are unremarkable. Her wbc is 17,000. Her blood pressure is 80/40 and HR is 120. She is afebrile. You examine her and she is fairly tender in the epigastric area. The most appropriate next step is:
   a.  Start IVF's and get an U/S
   b.  Start IVF's and get a CT scan
   c.  Start IVF's and go to OR
   d.  Start IVF's and go to MRI

> **Answer a.** The most appropriate initial steps in a patient with pancreatitis is to start giving them IV hydration (can lose a lot of volume with pancreatitis) and rule out gallstones as a source of the pancreatitis.
>
> If there was a dilated common bile duct or stone in the common bile duct on U/S, you would go with ERCP, sphincterotomy, and stone extraction.
>
> A CT scan would be useful to check for complications of pancreatitis, but it is not the best study for the diagnosis of gallstones.

419. You start IVF's on the patient and get an abdominal ultrasound which just shows normal anatomy. Five days later, the patient starts to worsen, so you place a central line (CVP 15) and have to start pressors (levophed) to keep her pressure up. You also have to intubate her for respiratory distress. She continues to worsen. You start broad spectrum antibiotics. At this point, you should:
   a.  Get an abdominal CT
   b.  Get an MRI
   c.  OR for laparotomy
   d.  Continue current management

**Answer a.** This patient is worsening clinically so prophylactic antibiotics are indicated. Patients with severe pancreatitis or those who are worsening clinically should have an abdominal CT scan to check for complications such as an abscess or infected pancreatitis.

420. The abdominal CT scan shows that 80% of the pancreas does not light up with IV contrast. You do not see any air bubbles or abscess pockets. The most appropriate next step is:
    a. Whipple
    b. Necrotic debridement
    c. Percutaneous drain
    d. Continue current management

**Answer d.** Sterile necrosis is left alone. Removing sterile necrotic material has not been shown to affect outcomes.

If gas were present in the necrotic pancreas (a sign of infected necrotic pancreas), you would go in and debride the area (or perhaps try to get a sample of the fluid 1$^{st}$ to make sure it was truly infected).

If an abscess were present, percutaneous drainage is likely not to work. These patients generally need open debridement of the abscess area. Leave drains.

421. A 50 yo woman with a pancreatic mass in the tail of the pancreas develops watery diarrhea and hypokalemia. The most likely diagnosis is:
    a. Glucagonoma
    b. Gastrinoma
    c. Somatostatinoma
    d. VIPoma

**Answer d.** Watery diarrhea and hypokalemia (without concomitant gastric ulcer disease) is most consistent with VIPoma.

The diarrhea associated with VIPoma will <u>not</u> get better with proton pump inhibitors whereas the diarrhea found with gastrinoma will get better with proton pump inhibitors.

422. A 50 yo woman with a pancreatic mass in the head of the pancreas has a stomach ulcer and persistent diarrhea. The most likely diagnosis is:
    a.  Glucagonoma
    b.  Gastrinoma
    c.  Somatostatinoma
    d.  VIPoma

**Answer b.** The most likely diagnosis is gastrinoma.

423. The secretin test in the above patient would likely show:
    a.  Increase in gastrin with administration
    b.  Decrease in gastrin with administration
    c.  No change in gastrin
    d.  Decreased lipase secretion

**Answer a.** The secretin test in patients with gastrinoma will show an increase in serum gastrin with administration of secretin.

424. In normal individuals, the secretin test would likely show:
    a.  Increase in gastrin with administration
    b.  Decrease in gastrin with administration
    c.  No change in gastrin
    d.  Decreased lipase secretion

**Answer b.** In normal individuals, serum gastrin secretion and HCL should decrease.

425. A 50 yo woman with a pancreatic mass develops diabetes and severe migrating, erythematous skin lesions. The most likely diagnosis is:
   a. Glucagonoma
   b. Gastrinoma
   c. Somatostatinoma
   d. VIPoma

   **Answer a.** Development of diabetes and a migrating, erythematous skin lesion is most consistent with glucagonoma.

426. The previous patient is noted to have an isolated 5 cm liver metastasis on pre-op CT scan (confirmed with biopsy). The pancreatic mass is located in the head of the pancreas and looks resectable. The most appropriate therapy is:
   a. Nothing
   b. 5-fluorouracil and XRT
   c. Morphine drip
   d. Resection of the pancreatic mass and the liver metastases

   **Answer d.** Debulking surgery is effective palliative treatment for functional endocrine tumors so resecting the liver mass is indicated if the primary could also be resected.

   Non-endocrine tumors (i.e. adenocarcinoma) of the pancreas with a liver metastasis would be considered unresectable and you would not perform a resection.

427. A 50 yo woman with an unresectable pancreatic mass has severe abdominal pain. Effective relief of this pain can be achieved with:
   a. Celiac plexus injection and block
   b. Bilateral sympathectomy
   c. Vagotomy
   d. Mesenteric plexus injection and block

**Answer a.** Celiac plexus injection and block can be effective therapy for patients with unresectable pancreatic lesions.


428. The right gastric artery is normally a branch off the:
    a. Gastroduodenal artery
    b. Right gastro-epiploic artery
    c. Pancreaticoduodenal artery
    d. Proper hepatic artery


**Answer d.** The right gastric artery is most commonly a branch of the proper hepatic artery.


429. You are performing a pancreaticoduodenal resection in a patient with a pancreatic head mass. You attempt to pass your finger behind the pancreas from below and get a large amount of blood return when you remove it. You place pressure on the neck of the pancreas to tamponade the bleeding which seems to control it. You have most likely injured the:
    a. Aorta
    b. Inferior vena cava
    c. Celiac artery
    d. Superior mesenteric vein


**Answer d.** The superior mesenteric vein lies directly behind the neck of the pancreas and is the structure most likely injured when trying to get behind the neck of the pancreas.


430. Most significant risk factor for pancreatic adenocarcinoma is:
    a. Tobacco
    b. Alcohol
    c. High fat diet
    d. Nitrosamines

**Answer a.** The most significant risk factor for the development of pancreatic cancer is tobacco use.

431. Treatment for intractable abdominal pain from chronic pancreatitis with a dilated pancreatic duct is usually:
   a. Percutaneous drainage
   b. Resection
   c. Lateral pancreatico-jejunostomy
   d. No operative therapies are available

   **Answer c.** Patients with chronic pancreatitis and intractable abdominal pain may benefit from lateral pancreatico-jejunostomy (Puestow procedure) if the pancreatic duct is greater than 8 mm.

432. Treatment for intractable abdominal pain from chronic pancreatitis with a normal pancreatic duct is usually:
   a. Percutaneous drainage
   b. Resection
   c. Lateral pancreatico-jejunostomy
   d. No operative therapies are available

   **Answer b.** Resection may be indicated in patient with intractable abdominal pain from pancreatitis.

433. A 55 yo man with significant ETOH abuse has an acute episode of pancreatitis. He gets a CT scan 2 weeks after the episode and is found to have a pancreatic pseudocyst. His pancreatitis has resolved and he is currently having mild symptoms of abdominal pain. The next appropriate action is:
   a. Percutaneous drainage
   b. Resection
   c. Follow conservatively
   d. Cysto-gastrostomy

187

**Answer c.** You should not operate on pancreatic pseudocysts unless they are mature (> 3 months) and are either persistently causing symptoms or are growing.

434. The above patient comes to your clinic in 3 months. You get a CT scan and the cyst is still the same size. He is not having any symptoms. The next appropriate action is:
    a. Percutaneous drainage
    b. Resection
    c. Follow conservatively
    d. Cysto-gastrostomy

**Answer c.** Because the cyst is not causing any symptoms and is not growing, the treatment of choice is to follow the lesion.

435. The above patient comes back again in 6 months with increased abdominal pain and an abdominal CT scan shows the lesion is now larger in size. You get an ERCP and the lesion has a connection to the pancreatic duct. The next appropriate action is:
    a. Percutaneous drainage
    b. Resection
    c. Follow conservatively
    d. Cysto-gastrostomy

**Answer d.** Once you determine that the pseudocyst is causing symptoms warranting intervention, get an ERCP to see if the pseudocyst has a connection with the pancreatic duct (it most likely does).

If it does not have a connection with the pancreatic duct, you can consider just percutaneous drainage which will treat some pancreatic pseudocysts which do not have a connection with pancreatic duct.

Most likely there was going to be a connection with the pancreatic duct (since the pseudocyst is getting bigger) and this patient needs either a percutaneous or open cystogastrostomy.

436. What is the only pancreatic enzyme secreted in active form?
    a. Amylase
    b. Trypsin
    c. Lipase
    d. Pepsin

**Answer a.** Amylase

437. A 55 yo woman undergoes pancreaticoduodenectomy for adenocarcinoma of the pancreas. Post-op day 7 she complains of increasing abdominal pain, nausea, and vomiting. The most appropriate next step in management is:
    a. Reglan
    b. Erythromycin
    c. Ultrasound
    d. MRI

**Answer c.** Although delayed gastric emptying could be the potential cause of this patient's symptoms (which would be treated with Reglan) you need to rule out a more serious problem such as a pancreatic duct leak, biliary system leak, or an abscess.

438. You obtain an ultrasound in the above patient and you see a large fluid collection anterior to the pancreas (9 x 9 cm). The most appropriate next step in management is:
    a. Percutaneous drainage and send the fluid for amylase, lipase, cytology, and other diagnostic tests
    b. Reglan
    c. Octreotide
    d. Nothing

**Answer a.** You should place a percutaneous drain and send the fluid off for amylase, lipase, and other diagnostic tests. This is suspicious for a pancreatic duct leak.

439. The fluid comes back with an amylase of 10,000. The most appropriate step in management is:
    a.  NPO, octreotide, TPN, follow drainage output
    b.  Re-operation with revision of the pancreatic anastomosis
    c.  Broad spectrum antibiotics
    d.  Nothing

**Answer a.** Now that you have placed a percutaneous drain, you have a controlled pancreatic fistula. The vast majority of these resolve on their own with conservative management which consists of octreotide, NPO status, and TPN.

# Spleen

440. Certain genetic disorders may require splenectomy to prevent the premature destruction of blood elements. The most common congenital abnormality requiring splenectomy:
   a. Hereditary spherocytosis
   b. Hereditary elliptocytosis
   c. Protein kinase deficiency
   d. Beta thalassemia minor

   **Answer a.** The most common congenital abnormality requiring splenectomy is hereditary spherocytosis.

441. Certain genetic disorders may require splenectomy to prevent the premature destruction of blood elements. Excluding genetic disorders which involve membrane proteins, the most common congenital abnormality requiring splenectomy is:
   a. Hereditary elliptocytosis
   b. G6PD deficiency
   c. Pyruvate kinase deficiency
   d. Hereditary spherocytosis

   **Answer c.** The most common non-membrane protein congenital abnormality requiring splenectomy is pyruvate kinase deficiency.

442. The most common non-traumatic condition requiring splenectomy:

   a. Idiopathic thrombocytopenic purpura (ITP)
   b. Thrombotic thrombocytopenic purpura (TTP)
   c. Hereditary spherocytosis
   d. Pyruvate kinase deficiency

   **Answer a.** The most common non-traumatic indication for splenectomy is ITP.

443. Continued destruction of blood elements following splenectomy can be related to an accessory spleen. The most common location of an accessory spleen is:
    a. Liver
    b. Kidney
    c. Adrenal gland
    d. Splenic hilum

**Answer d.** The most common location of an accessory spleen is the splenic hilum.

444. All of the following are characteristic of idiopathic thrombocytopenic purpura except:
    a. Enlarged spleen
    b. Anti-platelet antibodies
    c. In children < 10, this often resolves without further treatment
    d. The primary therapy is steroids

**Answer a.** ITP patients have normal spleens.

ITP involves anti-platelet antibodies which destroy platelets, leading to bleeding diatheses.

ITP in children under 10 usually resolves spontaneously.

The primary treatment is steroids.

Splenectomy is indicated if medical therapy fails.

Splenectomy removes the source of the IgG (B cells in the spleen).

445. All of the following are characteristic of thrombotic
thrombocytopenic purpura except:
    a.  Enlarged spleen
    b.  Loss of platelet inhibition
    c.  Splenectomy is usually indicated
    d.  The primary therapy is plasmapheresis

**Answer c.** TTP involves enlargement of the spleen.

There is loss of platelet inhibition with subsequent thrombosis
and loss of platelets.

Splenectomy is rarely indicated.

The primary therapy is plasmapheresis.

446. The splenic artery:
    a.  Is a branch of the left gastro-epiploic
    b.  Is a branch of the left gastric
    c.  Is a branch of the right gastric
    d.  Is a branch of the celiac axis

**Answer d.** The splenic artery is a branch off the celiac axis.

447. A 3 yo undergoes splenectomy for hereditary spherocytosis. Six
weeks later, the child returns to the emergency room with a fever
of 104, chills, rigors, and a systolic blood pressure of 60. The
child's white blood cell count is 20 All of the following are true of
the child's most likely condition except:
    a.  The condition is more common in patients who undergo
splenectomy for malignancy or hematologic disease
compared to trauma
    b.  The most common organism involved is N. meningitides
    c.  Children less then 5 years of age undergoing splenectomy
are at higher risk
    d.  The condition is due to a specific lack of immunity to
capsulated organisms

**Answer b.** Post-splenectomy sepsis syndrome is very rare after splenectomy. It occurs more commonly in patients undergoing splenectomy for non-traumatic indications.

The most common organism involved in PSSS is strep pneumoniae.

Children < 5 are at higher risk.

The condition is due to a specific lack of immunity to capsulated organisms (H. influenza, N meningitides, S. pneumoniae).

## Small bowel

448. A patient with a liver metastasis related to a small bowel carcinoid tumor develops flushing and diarrhea. These symptoms are most likely caused by:
   a. Epinephrine
   b. Serotonin
   c. Bradykinin
   d. ACTH

**Answer b.** Serotonin is released from carcinoid tumors.

Usually, carcinoid syndrome does not develop because the liver breaks down the serotonin before it goes systemic.

Metastases to the liver, however, can secrete serotonin that is not metabolized.

In patients with suspected carcinoid, 5-HIAA (a breakdown product of serotonin) can be measured in the urine.

449. The previous patient undergoes resection of a small bowel carcinoid involving an isolated liver metastasis. Two years later the patient develops vague abdominal complaints but you cannot identify any new lesions on CT scan. The best study to look for recurrent carcinoid tumor is:
   a. HIDA scan
   b. MIBG scan
   c. Octreotide scan
   d. MRI

**Answer c.** Octreotide scan is the most sensitive diagnostic test for the detection of a carcinoid tumor not apparent on CT scan.

450. You operate on a 25 yo man for presumed appendicitis and find a
1 cm tumor at the tip of the appendix. Pathology comes back on
the tumor as carcinoid. The most appropriate next step in
management is:
    a.  Right hemicolectomy
    b.  Close
    c.  XRT post-op
    d.  Chemotherapy post-op

**Answer b.** (see below)

451. You operate on a 25 yo man for presumed appendicitis and find a
2.5 cm tumor at the tip of the appendix. Pathology comes back on
the tumor as carcinoid. The most appropriate next step in
management is:
    a.  Right hemicolectomy
    b.  Close
    c.  XRT post-op
    d.  Chemotherapy post-op

**Answer a.** Appendectomy is adequate treatment for carcinoid
tumors localized to the appendix as long as they are less than
2 cm, not at the base, and there is no evidence of metastatic
disease.

If the above criteria are not met, you need to perform a right
hemi-colectomy.

452. You perform laparoscopy on a 25 yo man for presumed
appendicitis and find terminal ileitis not involving the cecal area.
The ileitis area is non-obstructing. The most appropriate next step
in management is:
    a.  Appendectomy
    b.  Close
    c.  Place a drain
    d.  Ileal resection

**Answer a.** Patients with presumed appendicitis but instead have terminal ileitis not involving the cecum should undergo appendectomy so that confusion of ileitis with appendicitis will not occur in the future.

If the cecum is involved in the ileitis, leave the appendix (high risk for leak).

453.Concerning short gut syndrome, all of the following are true except:
  a.   This is a clinical diagnosis of inability to absorb enough water and nutritional elements to be off TPN
  b.   The length of bowel in general needs to be at least 75 cm if there is no iliocecal valve
  c.   The length of bowel in general needs to be at least 50 cm if the iliocecal valve is present
  d.   The length of bowel needs to be at least 150 cm if there is no iliocecal valve

**Answer d.** Short gut syndrome is a clinical diagnosis of inability to maintain appropriate hydration and nutrition without the use of TPN.

In general though, the length of bowel needs to be at least 50 cm with the ilio-cecal valve and at least 75 cm without the ileal-cecal valve to avoid TPN.

197

## Colon and Rectum

454. A 60 yo man undergoes open cholecystectomy for cholecystitis and requires increased narcotics to control his pain. Five days later, he develops severe abdominal distension and pain. You get a plain film and the colon is 12 cm at the cecum. The most appropriate next step in this patient is:
   a.  Cecostomy
   b.  Colectomy
   c.  Colonoscopy
   d.  Nothing

   **Answer c.** Ogilvie's syndrome is pseudo-obstruction of the colon. It is associated with opiates, bed-ridden patients, infections, and trauma. These patients can get massively dilated colons.

   Treatment involves checking electrolytes (K, Mg), stopping drugs that slow the gut (i.e. narcotics) and colonoscopy to decompress the colon.

   Some suggest placing a rectal tube after decompression however the success of this is variable.

   Neostigmine has been used to treat this with varied results.

   If colonoscopy fails to decompress, proceed with cecostomy.

455. In an average male patient, the most distal extent of a rectal cancer which still allows for a low anterior resection with an appropriate margin is:
   a.  8 cm from the anal verge
   b.  6 cm from the anal verge
   c.  4 cm from the anal verge
   d.  2 cm from the anal verge

**Answer b.** The most distal extent of a rectal tumor which would still allow a 2 cm margin is about 6 cm from the anal verge.

Approximately 2 cm from the anal verge is the dentate line.

Approximately 2 cm from the dentate line is the levator ani muscles.

You need a 2 cm rectal cuff which will be resected with the end to end stapler (you need to send the donut in the stapler to path because this is part of your margin).

These distances vary from patient to patient.

In general, it is easier to perform low anterior resections in women compared to men because their pelvic bones are wider.

456. A 50 yo man undergoes low anterior resection followed by chemo-XRT. Six weeks after chemotherapy there is severe proctitis and bleeding from his rectum. He has required several transfusions for the problem. The best therapy for this patient is:
    a. Angio-embolization of the rectal arteries
    b. Abdomino-perineal resection
    c. Formalin fixation of the rectum
    d. Antibiotics

**Answer c.** Radiation proctitis leading to severe bleeding is best treated with formalin fixation of the rectum.

457. A 55 yo man undergoes low anterior resection of a low rectal cancer returns to clinic 6 months later with constipation. You perform anoscopy in the office and notice a mass at the previous suture line. Biopsies show adenocarcinoma. After a metastatic disease work-up, the next appropriate step is:
    a. Do nothing
    b. Chemotherapy w/ Leucovorin

    c.    5000 rads of XRT
    d.    Abdominal perineal resection

**Answer d.** Recurrence at the suture line following low anterior resection demands abdomino-perineal resection unless the patient has metastatic disease that precludes surgery. You should perform a thorough metastatic work-up in patients with recurrent cancer (Abdominal/Pelvic CT, CXR, LFT's, and CEA in this patient).

458. When performing an abdominal perineal resection, the vessels located in the lateral stalks are:
    a.    Middle rectal arteries
    b.    Superior rectal arteries
    c.    Superior sigmoidal arteries
    d.    Inferior sigmoidal arteries

**Answer a.** The middle rectal arteries are in the lateral stalks.

459. Ten days after a low anterior resection, your patient develops fever, a white blood cell count of 19,000, and mild abdominal tenderness. Your order a CT scan of the abdomen and pelvis which shows an 8 x 8 cm fluid collection near your anastomosis. The next appropriate step is:
    a.    Re-exploration and repair of the leak at the anastomosis
    b.    Percutaneous drainage
    c.    Abdominal perineal resection
    d.    Takedown of the anastomosis with placement of colostomy and Hartman's pouch

**Answer b.** This patient most likely has a leak from his anastomosis and subsequent abscess formation. Because the patient is not clinically septic and because it has been over 7 days since his surgery (bad time to re-operate because adhesions are starting to form but are not yet mature), the best move is to place a percutaneous drain.

460. Five days after a low anterior resection, your patient develops feculent brown drainage (1500 cc) from his abdominal wound. The next appropriate step is:
    a. Re-exploration and primary repair of the leak at the anastomosis
    b. Percutaneous drainage
    c. Abdominal perineal resection
    d. Takedown of the anastomosis with placement of colostomy and Hartman's pouch

**Answer d.** Because of the large amount of brown drainage (stool) and it being less than 7 days since his first surgery, you should proceed with re-exploration.

Because of the likelihood that there is going to be a lot of contamination, the best move in this patient is takedown of the anastomosis with placement of a colostomy and a Hartman's pouch.

If this patient had just a small leak and the area was not significantly contaminated, you could consider primary repair of the leak and placement of a diverting iliostomy. This, however, would be a very unlikely scenario in the above scenario.

461. Six hours after a low anterior resection, your patient has a fever of 41 degrees Celsius and develops gray, foul smelling drainage from his wound. The next appropriate step in management is:
    a. Make sure the patient is in cefazolin
    b. Abd CT
    c. Ostomy bag
    d. Re-exploration

**Answer d.** High fever early post-op with gray, foul smelling drainage is worrisome for clostridium perfringens (gram

201

positive rods) infection. The patient needs to be re-explored with debridement of the wound if infection is present.

This patient is at high risk for myonecrosis and fascitis.

462. Ten days after a low anterior resection, your patient develops clear yellow drainage from his wound. You send the fluid off and the creatnine is 40. Abdominal CT shows a fluid collection in the pelvis. The next appropriate step is:
   a. Re-exploration and repair
   b. Ostomy bag over the wound
   c. Long term urinary catheter
   d. Percutaneous drainage

**Answer d.** Most likely, this patient had transection of the ureter during the pelvic dissection. Although the temptation is to immediately operate on this patient, because it is over 7 days since the 1$^{st}$ surgery, you should wait.

Place a percutaneous drain and repair the ureteral injury in 6-8 weeks.

463. A 20 yo man comes to your office 8 weeks after an elective total proctocolectomy, J pouch formation, and loop iliostomy for familial adenomatous polyposis. He is here for consultation for iliostomy takedown. The most appropriate next step is this patient's management is:
   a. UGI series
   b. Upper endoscopy
   c. Abdominal CT
   d. Barium enema

**Answer d.** Before taking down this patients loop iliostomy, you need to make sure the ilio-anal anastomosis is not strictured. The best way to assess this is with a barium enema.

464. A 30 yo man with thickened sigmoid colon and diverticula presents with recurrent urinary tract infections. The most likely diagnosis is:
   a. adenocarcinoma
   b. squamous cell carcinoma
   c. carcinoid
   d. diverticulitis

   **Answer d.** Because of this patient's age and the fact he has diverticula, the most likely diagnosis is diverticulitis with colo-vesicle fistula.

465. A 65 yo man with thickened sigmoid colon and no diverticuli presents with pneumoturia, the most likely diagnosis is:
   a. adenocarcinoma
   b. squamous cell carcinoma
   c. carcinoid
   d. diverticulitis

   **Answer a.** Because of the patient's age and lack of diverticuli, the most likely diagnosis is adenocarcinoma with colo-vesicle fistula.

466. A 60 yo man undergoes right colectomy for adenocarcinoma. The final pathology report states the tumor invaded the muscularis propria and there was tumor in 2 of the mesenteric lymph nodes. What is the pathologic TNM classification of this cancer?
   a. T1, N0, MO
   b. T1, N1, MO
   c. T2, N0, M0
   d. T2, N1, M0

   **Answer d.** Invasion of the muscularis propria makes it T2. Involvement of 2 nodes makes it N1. The patient is T2N1M0.

T1: into submucosa
T2: into muscularis propria.
T3: into sub-serosa or non-peritonealized fat if no serosa
present.
T4: completely through serosa or into adjacent
organs/structures

N0: nodes negative
N1: 1–3 nodes positive
N2: ≥4 nodes positive
M1: distant metastases

467. What stage is this cancer?
    a.   Stage I
    b.   Stage II
    c.   Stage III
    d.   Stage IV

**Answer c.** The cancer is T2N1M0, so it is stage III.

Stage I: T1-2,N0,M0
Stage II: T3-4,N0,M0
Stage III: any N1 disease
Stage IV: any M1 disease

468. For the above question, following resection what is the most
appropriate next step?
    a.   5-FU and Leucovorin
    b.   Chemo-XRT
    c.   XRT
    d.   Nothing

**Answer a.** Because there was nodal involvement, this patient
is stage III and needs chemotherapy (5-FU and Leucovorin).

469. A 55 yo man is undergoing sigmoid resection for adenocarcinoma and you discover a mass in the liver. The patient did not have a pre-operative abdominal CT scan. Intra-operative ultrasound reveals the tumor is deep in the right lobe and you would have to perform a lobectomy for resection. The best management for this patient would be:

    a. Finish sigmoid resection and perform right liver lobectomy
    b. Close without performing sigmoid resection
    c. Sigmoid resection with biopsy of the lesion
    d. Right liver lobectomy only

**Answer c.** Because it would require a major liver resection to get the metastasis out and because you have not done an extensive metastatic disease work-up, you should just perform the sigmoid resection.

After that, do a complete metastatic work-up in 6-8 weeks and then bring the patient back for resection of the hepatic lesion if the metastatic disease work-up is negative.

In general, metastases do not metastasize, so the 6-8 week interval is not likely to affect the patient's prognosis.

If this were just a small metastases (< 1 cm deep) and easily taken out with a wedge resection, removing it would be OK at the time of the sigmoid resection.

Removal of isolated liver metastases for colon cancer has a 25% 5 year survival.

Metastases to the liver are fed primarily by the hepatic artery (which would be the route of intra-arterial chemotherapy or embolization).

470. In patients who have undergone total proctocolectomy for FAP, the most common cause of death is:

    a. Liver cancer
    b. Adrenal cancer
    c. Duodenal cancer

d.   Small bowel cancer

**Answer c.** Patients with FAP can also develop duodenal polyps which should be followed and removed. These polyps have malignant potential.

471. A 55 yo man is undergoing a right colectomy for adenocarcinoma. When you enter the abdomen, the tumor appears to be invading about 0.5 cm into the liver based on intra-operative ultrasound. The best management for this patient would be:
  a.   Right hemicolectomy only and leave the liver component
  b.   En bloc right hemicolectomy including the portion of the cancer invading the liver
  c.   Wedge the liver lesion out only
  d.   close

**Answer b.** Direct invasion of another structure requires en bloc resection if at all possible.

472. The most common location for colon cancer is:
  a.   Right colon
  b.   Transverse colon
  c.   Descending colon
  d.   Sigmoid colon

**Answer d.** The most common location for colon cancer is the sigmoid colon.

473. A 65 yo patient has T3N1M0 rectal adenocarcinoma 8 cm from the anal verge (based on abdominal and pelvic CT scan, trans-rectal ultrasound, and biopsies of the lesion itself as well as a node identified during the TRUS). He undergoes pre-op chemo therapy with Leucovorin and 5000 rads of XRT. You re-stage the patient,

(including biopsies of the rectum and the previous node) and you cannot find any residual tumor. The next step in management is:
    a.   Sigmoidoscopy every 6 months
    b.   Low anterior resection
    c.   Abdomino-perineal resection
    d.   No further follow-up or resection

**Answer b.** Even though you cannot find any residual tumor, the standard of care is still resection. Somewhere around 15-20% will still have cancer present on final pathology.

This would also be the case if the patient needed an APR, although some groups are following these patients.

474. A 50 man presents with pain on defecation and some red streaking after bowel movements. You perform anoscopy which feels tight and notice some piled up anoderm posteriorly in the midline. The initial treatment for this patient is:
    a.   Sitz baths, lidocaine jelly, stool softeners, nitrate paste
    b.   Abdomino-perineal resection
    c.   Low anterior resection
    d.   Lateral subcutaneous internal sphincterotomy

**Answer a.** The initial treatment of anal fissure (the piled up anoderm is the sentinel pile associated with these lesions) is medical with Sitz baths, lidocaine jelly, stool softeners, and nitrate paste.

475. The above therapy doesn't work. The next step in management is:
    a.   Abdomino-perineal resection
    b.   Low anterior resection
    c.   Lateral subcutaneous internal sphincterotomy
    d.   Hemorrhoidectomy

**Answer c.** The treatment of choice for anal fissures refractory to medical therapy is lateral subcutaneous internal sphincterotomy.

476. If the fissure was located laterally instead of posteriorly, what disease should be ruled out?
    a. Crohn's disease
    b. Ulcerative colitis
    c. Gardner's Disease
    d. FAP

**Answer a.** Patients with lateral or anterior fissures need to have Crohn's disease and anal cancer ruled out.

Ulcerative colitis does not involve the anus.

Crohn's disease can involve the anus.

477. A 50 yo man has severe hematochezia requiring 6 units of blood in 12 hours. The bleeding is ongoing. His blood pressure in 110/60 and his HR is 110. You do not find anything on anoscopy. You place an NG tube and get back bile but no blood. The next appropriate step is:
    a. Emergent subtotal colectomy
    b. Angiography
    c. Tagged red blood cell scan
    d. Colonoscopy

**Answer b.** This would be considered massive bleeding because of the transfusion requirement. You are unlikely to find anything on colonoscopy because there is too much blood.

You should not go directly to the OR for a sub-total colectomy unless the patient was hypotensive despite aggressive resuscitation attempts. Try to localize the area 1st.

Angiography is the best choice, which will localize the lesion.
Then take the patient to the OR for colectomy at the
appropriate location.

478. Angiogram fails to localize the bleed in the above patient. While
in the angio suite, the patient starts bleeding again. Despite
another 6 units of blood his pressure is 70/40 and his HR is 125.
The next appropriate step is:
   a. Emergent subtotal colectomy
   b. Angiography
   c. Tagged red blood cell scan
   d. Colonoscopy

   **Answer a.** This scenario forces your hand to performing a
   sub-total colectomy.

479. A 50 yo man presents with mild hematochezia. EGD is negative.
You perform anoscopy and colonoscopy, but can't find the
problem area. The patient continues to have melana and requires
intermittent transfusion (1 unit rbc's every 2-3 days). The most
sensitive test to find the area that is bleeding is:
   a. Exploration
   b. Angiography
   c. Tagged red blood cell scan
   d. Colonoscopy

   **Answer c.** Tagged red blood cell scan is the most sensitive
   test for lower GI bleeding (can detect 0.1 cc/min).

480. A 55 yo man has an episode of bleeding from diverticulosis (which
you saw with colonoscopy) in the sigmoid colon which resolves
with conservative management. He presents 2 weeks later with a
similar episode. The most appropriate next step is:
   a. Sigmoidectomy
   b. Conservative management

209

c.  Angiography
d.  Tagged rbc scan


**Answer a.** Recurrence of bleeding is an indication for surgery.


481. A 50 yo man presents with an anal mass. You biopsy it and it comes back as cloacogenic cancer. The most appropriate next step is:
    a.  Abdomino-perineal resection
    b.  Laser fulgration
    c.  Chemo-XRT
    d.  Low anterior resection


**Answer c.** The most appropriate treatment of squamous cell CA of the anus (cloacogenic CA is a variant of squamous cell CA) is the nigro protocol, which consists of 5-FU and mitomycin, plus XRT.


482. All of the following are true of hereditary non-polyposis colon cancer syndrome except:
    a.  Needs to be in 3 primary relatives, over 2 generations, with one person being less than 50 at the time of diagnosis of cancer
    b.  Cancers are right sided predominant
    c.  Ovarian, breast and stomach cancer can also occur in these patients
    d.  The patients have thousands of polyps


**Answer d.** These patients do not form thousands of polyps like FAP patients.

The colon cancers are right sided predominant and there is a predilection to ovarian, breast and stomach cancers.


210

The syndrome is caused by a defect in a mis-match repair enzyme.

483. A 75 yo woman from a nursing home presents with abdominal pain and distension. You get a plain film and the colon is very distended and looks like an 'ace of spades' pointing to the LLQ. She does not have peritoneal signs. The most appropriate next step in management is:
   a. Sigmoidoscopy
   b. Low anterior resection
   c. Abdomino-perineal resection
   d. Do nothing

**Answer a.** Given the presentation, this patient most likely has a sigmoid volvulus.

If a patient presents with sigmoid volvulus and peritoneal signs, you should not try sigmoidoscopy to straighten out the colon but proceed directly to the OR for either:

1) resection if the sigmoid colon is infarcted or

2) detorsion, close, colon prep, back for resection in 2 days if the colon is viable.

If the patient does not have peritoneal signs (such as the patient presented in the scenario), you should proceed with sigmoidoscopy. If that fails, go to the OR and follow the above pathway.

## Hernias

484. A 65 yo woman presents with a tender mass just below the inguinal ligament. This most likely represents:
    a.  An inguinal hernia
    b.  An obturator hernia
    c.  A ventral hernia
    d.  A femoral hernia

**Answer d.** A mass just below the inguinal ligament is most consistent with a femoral hernia.

Femoral canal boundaries are:
    Superior - inguinal ligament
    Inferior – pectineal ligament
    Medial – lacunar ligament (attaches to the pubis and connects the inguinal and pectineal ligaments)
    Lateral - femoral vein

485. During repair of a femoral hernia through an inguinal approach, you try to reduce the bowel but are unsuccessful. The most appropriate next step is:
    a.  Pull on the bowel until it gives
    b.  Resect the bowel through a femoral exploration
    c.  Divide the rectus muscle
    d.  Divide the inguinal ligament

**Answer d.** If you are unable to reduce the bowel for a femoral hernia through an inguinal approach, cut the inguinal ligament, reduce the bowel (making sure its viable $1^{st}$), and then repair the inguinal ligament.

486. The most commonly injured nerve with inguinal hernia repair is:

    a.  Ilio-inguinal nerve
    b.  Genitofemoral nerve

c.  Sciatic nerve
d.  Lumbosacral plexus nerves


**Answer a.** The most commonly injured nerve with inguinal hernia repair is the ilioinguinal nerve, which causes loss of the cremasteric reflex and ipsilateral thigh/scrotum numbness.


487. At reoperation for a recurrence of an inguinal hernia following laparoscopic repair, the most common location for the recurrent hernia is:
    a.  Lateral
    b.  Medial
    c.  Anterior
    d.  Posterior


**Answer b.** The most common location for breakdown of a laparoscopic hernia repair is the medial portion of the mesh. The usual cause is that the mesh is too small. The other reason is failure to appropriately attach the mesh medially.


488. The organ most commonly found in a sliding hernia in women is:
    a.  Small bowel
    b.  Cecum
    c.  Spleen
    d.  Ovary


**Answer d.** The organ most commonly involved in a sliding hernia in a woman is the ovary (or fallopian tubes).

With a sliding hernia, a visceral wall makes up part of the sac.


489. The organ most commonly found in a sliding hernia in a man is:
    a.  Small bowel
    b.  Cecum

213

    c.   Spleen
    d.   Stomach

**Answer b.** The organ most commonly involved in a sliding hernia in a man is the cecum (or sigmoid colon).

490. The most common complication following inguinal hernia repair is:
    a.   Urinary retention
    b.   Recurrence
    c.   Bleeding
    d.   Infection

**Answer a.** The most common complication following an inguinal hernia repair is urinary retention. Risk factors include males, increased narcotic requirement and age.

491. A 65 yo woman presents with a tender medial thigh mass. The pain increases with internal rotation of the thigh. This most likely represents:
    a.   An inguinal hernia
    b.   An obturator hernia
    c.   A ventral hernia
    d.   A femoral hernia

**Answer b.** The scenario presented is most consistent with an obturator hernia. The Howship-Romberg sign is pain with internal rotation of the thigh, which is characteristic of an obturator hernia.

**Urology (also see Trauma Section)**

492. All of the following are true of renal cell carcinoma except:
    a.  They can synthesize erythropoietin
    b.  They have a predilection to growing into the ICV
    c.  When growing into the IVC, IVC reconstruction is often needed
    d.  The classic presentation is pain, abdominal mass, and hematuria

    **Answer c.** Although these tumors have a predilection for IVC invasion, they usually do not attach to the walls and can be plucked out of the IVC at the time of nephrectomy.

493. All of the following are true of bladder cancer except:
    a.  The most common is transitional cell carcinoma
    b.  Schistosomiasis infection is associated with squamous cell carcinoma of the bladder
    c.  Transitional cell carcinoma limited to the submucosa can be treated with intra-vesicle BCG or trans-urethral resection
    d.  Transitional cell carcinoma with invasion of the muscle (T2) is best treated with wedge resection

    **Answer d.** Transitional cell CA with muscle invasion requires total cystectomy and formation of an ileal conduit.

494. The seminiferous vesicles are connected to:
    a.  The epididymis
    b.  The urethra
    c.  The vas deferens
    d.  The ureters

    **Answer c.** The seminiferous vesicles are connected to the vas deferens.

## Gynecology

495. A 25 yo woman complains of cyclical rectal bleeding, You
     perform anoscopy and find a blue mass at 5 cm above the dentate
     line (3 cm above the levators) Given the likely diagnosis, all of
     the following are true except:
     a. Symptoms related to this condition are dysmenorrhea,
        infertility, and dyspareunia
     b. Ovaries are the most common site
     c. This lesion requires low anterior resection
     d. This lesion can be treated with hormonal manipulation

     **Answer c.** This patient has endometriosis, which is usually
     controlled with OCP's. A blue rectal mass in a young female
     patient who presents with rectal bleeding should alert you to
     endometriosis.

496. All of the following are true of ovarian cancer except:
     a. Ovarian cancer with peritoneal metastases is usually
        treated primarily with total abdominal hysterectomy,
        bilateral oophrectomy, resection of peritoneal metastases,
        and omentectomy
     b. Debulking therapy can be effective in these patients
     c. Risk factors include nulliparity, early menarche, and late
        menopause
     d. Risk factors for ovarian cancer include oral contraceptive
        pills

     **Answer d.** Use of oral contra-ceptive pills lowers the risk of
     ovarian cancer. The rest of the answers are true. Debulking
     therapy is effective for ovarian CA.

497. A 55 yo post-menopausal woman has a newly discovered ovarian
     cancer on the right side. Which of the following is false?
     a. Cancer found in both ovaries but not anywhere else is
        considered stage I disease

216

b. Debulking therapy can be effective in patients with large tumors that cannot be completely resected
c. The clear cell type of ovarian cancer has a very poor prognosis
d. In general, ovarian cancer in this population is treated by removing the ovary only

**Answer d.** Ovarian cancer is optimally treated with total abdominal hysterectomy and bilateral oophrectomy for all stages.

The decision tree is complicated in patients still in their child-bearing years who want children, in which limited resection may be considered based on how far spread the disease is, what type of tumor it is, and whether or not the woman still wants to have children.

The rest of the answers are true.

498. A 50 yo woman s/p total abdominal hysterectomy, bilateral oophrectomy, and chemo-XRT of the pelvis for ovarian cancer starts having stool come out of her vagina. Multiple biopsies of the area do not reveal any cancer, just fibrotic tissue and a 3 cm hole that is high in the vagina. The most appropriate management is:
a. XRT
b. Resection of involved rectum, primary closure of the vagina, and colostomy
c. Abdominal perineal resection
d. Rectal stent

**Answer b.** Benign complex (although you should check the path in this patient after repair) recto-vaginal fistulas are treated with resection of the involved rectum, closure of the vagina, and interposition of tissue such at omentum between the vagina and the rectum.

After resection, you can either place a colostomy with Hartman's pouch (or mucus fistula) with reconnection later or

217

you can reconnect at the primary surgery with placement of a loop iliostomy to be taken down at a later date.

Simple recto-vaginal fistulas (< 2.5 cm, low in the vagina, related usually to rectal trauma, <u>not</u> related to Crohn's or XRT) can be treated with rectal advancement flaps.

499. A 21 yo sexually active woman presents with abdominal pain and discharge. You perform a pelvic exam and she has cervical motion tenderness and discharge from her cervix. The most appropriate therapy is:
    a. Ceftriaxone and doxycycline
    b. Bactrim
    c. Vancomycin
    d. Levofloxacin

**Answer a.** This patient most likely has pelvic inflammatory disease related to Chlamydia or Gonorrhea. Treatment is with ceftriaxone and doxycycline.

You could get a smear to try and identify the culprit organism, but there is a chance the patient has multiple organisms and you are only finding one on smear. It is best to cover for both Chlamydia and Gonorrhea.

500. A 65 yo woman has stage II squamous cell carcinoma of the vulva. What is the most appropriate therapy?
    a. Radiation therapy
    b. Chemotherapy
    c. Resection of involved labia
    d. Bilateral labial resection

**Answer d.**

Stage I is vulvar cancer limited to one labia and is < 2 cm.

Stage II is > 2 cm.

Stage III involves nodes or invasive disease beyond the labia.

Treatment of stage I vulvar cancer is removal of the labia.

Treatment of stage II vulvar cancer is bilateral labial resection.

Treatment of stage III vulvar cancer is wide en bloc resection and nodal dissection.

501. A 50 yo post-menopausal woman is diagnosed with ovarian cancer. During laparoscopic evaluation, she has disease in both ovaries, however, all of your peritoneal biopsies, diaphragm biopsies and peritoneal washings are negative. What stage is this patient's cancer?
   a.  Stage I
   b.  Stage II
   c.  Stage III
   d.  Stage IV

   **Answer a.** Ovarian cancer limited to both ovaries is still stage I.

502. The above patient requires:
   a.  Oophrectomy and partial oophrectomy
   b.  Bilateral oophrectomy
   c.  Bilateral oophrectomy and salpingectomy
   d.  Total abdominal hysterectomy and bilateral oophrectomy

   **Answer d.** Even though the patient is stage I disease, she still needs a total abdominal hysterectomy and bilateral oophrectomy.

503. The most common type of ovarian tumor is:
   a.  Epithelial

219

b. Germ cell
c. Sex-cord
d. Lymphoma

**Answer a**. The most common type of ovarian cancer is epithelial.

504. A 28 yo old woman presents to the ER with severe abdominal pain, a distended abdomen, a systolic blood pressure of 60 despite 2 liters of lactated ringers, and a heart rate of 120. The hematocrit comes back at 18. The most appropriate next step is:
   a. Laparotomy
   b. FFP and go to the ICU
   c. Send a beta-HCG
   d. Abdominal CT scan

**Answer a.** Sometimes you can't wait for a diagnosis. The most appropriate step in this patient is to go to the OR and figure it out in there.

## Orthopaedics

505. A 20 yo man falls on an outstretched hand and now complains of tenderness in the "snuff box" of his right hand. You get an XR but it is negative. The most appropriate next step is:
   a. Spica cast up to the elbow, repeat films in 2 weeks
   b. Exploration
   c. Nothing
   d. Tape fingers together

   **Answer a.** Snuff box tenderness is worrisome for a scaphoid bone fracture. These fractures are hard to see on XR. They are at high risk for avascular necrosis.

   The treatment of a patient with snuff box tenderness and suspected scaphoid fracture is a cast up to the elbow with a follow-up XR in 2 weeks.

506. A 59 yo woman undergoes an abdomino-perineal resection which takes 12 hours. Post-operatively, you note she has a foot drop on the right. All of the following are true except:
   a. Proper patient positioning could have likely prevented this problem
   b. This patient should have a fasciotomy
   c. This problem is related to the common peroneal nerve
   d. A foot brace may benefit this patient

   **Answer b.** This patient likely suffered a peroneal nerve injury where the peroneal nerve wraps around the leg at the level of the fibula. This occurred from compression of this area while in the lithotomy position.

507. A 24 yo man suffers a supracondylar humeral fracture. Six hours after the event, the patient has his arm reduced and placed in a sling. Shortly afterwards, the patient develops severe forearm

221

swelling and pain. The arm is tense. You have trouble finding distal pulses. The most appropriate next step in management is:
   a.  Emergent open reduction and internal fixation
   b.  Emergency repair of the brachial artery
   c.  Angiogram and stent placement
   d.  Forearm fasciotomies

**Answer d.** Compartment syndrome (Volkmann's contracture in this case) can occur after the interruption of blood flow, a delay (4-6 hours), and then restoration of blood flow. This patient needs forearm fasciotomies to the volar and dorsal compartments.

508. The vessel primarily involved in the above injury is:
   a.  The radial artery
   b.  The ulnar artery
   c.  The brachial artery
   d.  The anterior interosseous artery

**Answer d.** The vessel involved in the above injury is the anterior interosseous artery.

509. Anterior dislocation of the shoulder is most likely to injure the:
   a.  Subclavian vein
   b.  Subclavian artery
   c.  Axillary nerve
   d.  Thoracic duct

**Answer c.** Anterior dislocation of the arm is most likely to injure the axillary nerve.

510. Posterior dislocation of the hip is most likely to injure the:
   a.  Femoral artery
   b.  Femoral vein

c.   Sciatic nerve
d.   Femoral nerve


**Answer c.** Posterior dislocation of the hip is most likely to injure the sciatic nerve.

## Pediatric Surgery

511. Treatment for a type I choledochal cyst is:
    a.  Careful follow-up
    b.  Cystogastrostomy
    c.  Cystoduodenostomy
    d.  Cyst resection and hepatic-jejunostomy

**Answer d.** Choledochal cysts need to be resected because of the risk of forming cancer in the cyst and the risk of cholangitis and pancreatitis.

512. The maximum barium column height and maximum air pressure when trying to reduce an intussusception are:
    a.  Column height 1 meter, air pressure 120 mmHg
    b.  Column height 2 meters, air pressure 240 mmHg
    c.  Column height 2 meters, air pressure 240 mmHg
    d.  Column height 2 meters, air pressure 240 mmHg

**Answer a.** The maximum column height of barium when trying to reduce an intussusception is 1 meter. The maximum air pressure if you are using an air contrast enema is 120 mmHg.

If the intussusception does not reduce with those maximums (can keep it there for about an hour), take the patient to the OR and do it manually.

You risk perforation if you go higher than these values.

513. In your office, you see a 1 year old with an undescended testicle on the left side. All of the following are true except:
    a.  Patients with un-descended testicles have a higher incidence of testicular cancer
    b.  This patient should have elective surgery as soon as possible

224

c. Chromosomal studies are indicated if both testicles are not in the scrotum
d. Division of the spermatic vessels is an acceptable method of gaining length on the testicle if it does not reach the scrotum

**Answer b.** Patients with unilateral undescended testicles should undergo repair at 2 years of age.

Chromosomal studies should be performed if both testicles are not in the scrotum.

If you cannot feel the testicle in the inguinal canal by age 2, you should get an MRI to find it.

These patients are at higher risk for testicular cancer compared to the rest of the population. Placing the testicle into the scrotum does not change this risk.

514. A 2 year old is brought into your office for an umbilical hernia. All of the following are true except:
   a. This patient should have surgery at about age 5 if the hernia fails to close
   b. This patient is at high risk for incarceration
   c. These hernias are increased in African-American patients
   d. These hernias are increased in premature patients

**Answer b.** Patients with umbilical hernias are at low risk for incarceration. Repair should be done at age 5 if the hernia has failed to close. Umbilical hernias are increased in African-American populations and premature infants.

515. A 2 year old is brought into your office with a bulge in his left groin. Your try to reduce the hernia but you are unsuccessful. All of the following are true except:
   a. This patient should have surgery at about age 5 if the hernia fails to close

b. This patient is at high risk for infarction
c. These hernias are more common in the right
d. These hernias are increased in premature patients

**Answer a.** Inguinal hernias should be repaired soon after they are discovered..

Incarcerated hernias (which is what this patient has) should be repaired the same day as discovery.

516. A newborn infant fails to pass meconium in the $1^{st}$ 24 hours of life and subsequently gets progressive abdominal distension. Your order plain films which show a distended colon. On exam, the child has an anus located in the proper position and on rectal exam there is explosive release of watery stool. The most appropriate next test is:
a. Upper GI series
b. Barium enema
c. Enteroclysis
d. Rectal biopsy

**Answer d.** The scenario is most consistent with Hirschsprung's disease. Diagnosis of Hirschsprung's Disease is made with rectal biopsy, which shows the absence of ganglion cells in the myenteric plexus.

517. A newborn infant fails to pass meconium in the $1^{st}$ 24 hours of life and subsequently gets progressive abdominal distension. Your order plain films which show distended loops of small bowel, but no air-fluid levels. The colon is totally decompressed. The transition point is in the RLQ. On exam, the child has an anus located in the proper position. The most appropriate next test is:
a. Upper GI series
b. Barium enema
c. Enteroclysis
d. Rectal biopsy

226

**Answer b.** The clinical scenario above is most consistent with meconium ileus. The obstruction occurs in the terminal ileum. No air-fluid levels form because the bowel contents stick to the bowel wall instead of pooling (thick meconium).

Barium enema can make the diagnosis as well as relieve the obstruction. N-acetylcysteine enemas work better than barium enemas for relieving the obstruction.

This infant also needs either a sweat chloride test or PCR for the Cl channel defect associated with cystic fibrosis.

518. A 3 week old infant who is otherwise healthy is brought to the emergency room for vomiting of greenish fluid. The most appropriate next test is:
   a. Upper GI series
   b. Barium enema
   c. Enteroclysis
   d. Rectal biopsy

**Answer a.** Bilious vomiting in any child in the first 2 years of life requires an upper GI series to rule out malrotation. This needs to be done emergently.

Malrotation can result in necrosis of the entire small bowel from volvulus and strangulation of the superior mesenteric artery.

Ladd's procedure (to treat malrotation) involves resection of the Ladd's band's, counter clockwise rotation of the bowel, appendectomy, and fixation of the cecum in the left lower quadrant.

519. A 3 week old male infant is brought to the emergency room for repeated forceful vomiting such that it hits the wall opposite the child. On exam, you notice a small protuberance in his right upper quadrant. The most appropriate next test is:

227

a. Upper GI series
b. Ultrasound
c. Enteroclysis
d. Abdominal CT scan

**Answer b.** Projectile vomiting and "olive" in the RUQ is most consistent with pyloric stenosis. Diagnosis is best with ultrasound (upper GI series if ultrasound not available).

Ultrasound criteria for pyloric stenosis are a pylorus ≥ 4 mm thick or ≥ 14 mm long.

Treatment is pyloromyotomy.

520. A newborn is found to be in severe respiratory distress immediately following birth. CXR shows loops of bowel filling the left chest. All of the following are true except:
   a. Patients with this problem have about a 50% survival overall
   b. The incidence of this problem is increased on the left side compared to right
   c. Both lungs in patients with this problem are often dysfunctional
   d. Patients with this problem require repair immediately after birth

**Answer d.** The above scenario is most consistent with congenital diaphragmatic hernia. This lesion is associated with about a 50% overall survival.

It is more common on the left (80%) and both lungs are usually dysfunctional (one from compression by the bowel and the dysfunction in the contralateral lung is not completely understood).

Pulmonary hypertension is frequent in this population.

Current treatment of choice in these children is stabilization with high frequency ventilation, ECMO, and/or inhaled NO before repair. Delayed repair after the patient is able to better tolerate surgery is thought to improve survival.

521. A 5 year old child (30 kg) is brought to the emergency room by his parents after being hit by a passing car. He is awake and alert, breathing 30 breaths per minute with clear lung sounds, has a heart rate of 110 and systolic blood pressure of 80 with abdominal tenderness. The nurse gets 2 large bore intravenous lines in. The next appropriate step is:
   a. Go to the operating room
   b. Abd CT scan
   c. Fluid bolus with 600 cc of lactated ringers
   d. Fluid bolus with 300 cc of lactated ringers

   **Answer c.** The proper initial fluid bolus in a child is 20 cc/kg of lactated ringers.

   The normal heart rate in a 5 yo is about 100 and normal SBP is about 90. This patient is in approximately class I shock.

522. A 15 year old boy develops sudden, severe scrotal pain and a high-riding right testicle. The next appropriate step is:
   a. Bilateral exploration of testicles through inguinal incision
   b. Unilateral exploration of testicle through inguinal incision
   c. Bilateral exploration of testicles through scrotal incision
   d. Unilateral exploration of testicle through scrotal incision

   **Answer c.** Treatment of choice for testicular torsion is to pexy the involved testicle if still viable (otherwise resection) and to pexy the contralateral testicle.

523. A newborn infant suffers from severe aspiration and choking with feeding. You try to place an NG tube and cannot get it down. CXR shows the NG tube stops in the mid-esophagus. The most likely diagnosis is:

   a.   Congenital diaphragmatic hernia
   b.   Omphalocele
   c.   Gastrochesis
   d.   Tracheo-esophageal fistula


   **Answer d.** The clinical scenario presented is most consistent
   with TE fistula.


524. The most common type of TE fistula is:
   a.   Type A
   b.   Type B
   c.   Type C
   d.   Type D


   **Answer c.** Type C TEF is the most common. This involves a
   proximal esophageal pouch and a distal TEF. You cannot
   pass an NGT because it gets held up in the pouch.


525. Treatment of the above problems generally involves:
   a.   right thoracotomy and end to end anastomosis
   b.   gastric replacement of the esophagus
   c.   colon replacement of the esophagus
   d.   jejunal replacement of the esophagus


   **Answer a.** Treatment of TEF generally involves a right
   thoracotomy and end to end anastomosis of the esophagus and
   closure of the trachea.


526. The most common post-op complication following TE fistula
   repair is:
   a.   Leak
   b.   Sepsis
   c.   Necrosis of the esophagus
   d.   Reflux

**Answer d.** A very frequent complication following repair of TEF's is the development of reflux disease necessitating a reflux procedure.

527. A 32 yo man presents with a painful testicular mass that has been present for about 3 months. All of the following are true except:
   a. This is unlikely to be testicular torsion
   b. The patient should have an orchiectomy via trans-scrotal approach
   c. The patient should have an orchiectomy via trans-inguinal approach
   d. The patient should have trans-scrotal percutaneous biopsy

**Answer c.** This most likely represents a testicular tumor. This is unlikely to be testicular torsion as it is a mass and has been present for 3 months (testicular torsion presents very acutely – within hours).

An important concept in these patients is that you do not want to disrupt the lymphatic plane in these patients, which means you do not want any scrotal incisions (or biopsies).

Treatment of choice of this mass is orchiectomy via trans-inguinal approach (the testicle is your biopsy specimen).

231

## Skin and soft tissue

528. A 45 yo woman presents to your office with a lump in her right
axilla that she has noticed for 3 months. She does not have any
constitutional symptoms and has had no recent infections. You
obtain a mammogram which is normal. A complete physical exam
reveals no other suspicious lesions. The mass is about 2 cm in
diameter, feels hard, and is not painful. There is no surrounding
erythema. The most appropriate next step is:
   a. Antibiotics
   b. Core needle biopsy
   c. Close follow-up
   d. Sentinel lymph node biopsy

   **Answer b.** This mass needs to be biopsied.

   Antibiotics are not indicated because there has been no
   antecedent illness and the mass is not inflammatory. Also it
   would be unusual for an inflammatory mass to last 3 months.

   Sentinel lymph node biopsy is indicated for primary lesions
   with clinically negative nodes.

   You could resect the mass (excisional biopsy) if the core
   needle biopsy was indeterminant.

529. You perform a core needle biopsy in the above patient and find it
is a lymph node. You send it to path and it comes back melanoma.
You cannot find any skin lesions on the patient's body. The most
appropriate next step is:
   a. Formal axillary lymph node dissection
   b. nothing
   c. Mastectomy
   d. Chemo-XRT only

   **Answer a.** There are a couple of possibilities with this
   scenario.

The first is that there is a melanoma primary somewhere in the patient and you cannot find it (some melanomas are non-pigmented).

Another possibility is that the primary melanoma has regressed spontaneously and the lymph nodes are all that is left of the disease.

The problem is that you do not know which category this patient falls into, so err on the side that will give the patient the best chance of survival, which is a formal axillary lymph node dissection.

Note that the dissection for melanoma is different than that for breast cancer. For melanoma, you are trying to remove all the disease which means you need to take the level I, II, and III lymph nodes.

With breast cancer, you only need to sample level I (some say level II as well) nodes. You are not trying to remove all the disease with breast cancer, you are merely staging the patient.

530. An appropriate margin for a 2 cm basal cell carcinoma on the forearm is:
    a.   0.5 cm
    b.   1 cm
    c.   2 cm
    d.   3 cm

**Answer a.** 0.3 to 0.5 cm margins are sufficient for basal cell carcinoma.

531. A 65 yo man has a 1 cm diameter dark colored lesion on his arm that looks different according to the patient. You perform a physical exam and find no other lesions. The next appropriate step is:
    a.   Resection with 1 cm margin
    b.   Punch biopsy

c. IL-2 therapy

d. Scrape top layer off and send to cytology

**Answer b.** Because you do not know if this is melanoma or not, resection with a margin is not indicated (also, margins are based on depth of lesion, not width).

IL-2 therapy would be indicated for metastatic disease.

Scraping off the top layer would be an inappropriate way of making the diagnosis because you would not be getting the depth of the lesion.

The best answer is punch biopsy (although you could also just resect the lesion without margins, and then go back for a re-resection if it turns out to be cancer).

532. The punch biopsy in the above patient comes back as melanoma that invades 2 mm deep. You perform a physical exam (axillary region) and find no clinically positive nodes. Metastatic work-up is negative. The most appropriate next step is:
   a. Sentinel lymph node biopsy and resection of the primary with 2 cm margin
   b. Axillary lymph node dissection and resection of the primary with 2 cm margin
   c. Sentinel lymph node biopsy and resection of the primary with 1 cm margin
   d. Axillary lymph node dissection and resection of the primary with a 1 cm margin

**Answer a.** Sentinel lymph node biopsy is indicated if the lesion is > 1 mm deep and the nodes are clinically negative.

Clinically positive nodes require axillary LN dissection.

A melanoma 2 mm (1-4 mm) deep requires a 2 cm margin with resection.

A melanoma < 1 mm requires a 1 cm margin.

A melanoma > 4 mm deep requires a 2-3 cm margin depending on location.

## Statistics

533. There were 172,000 new cases of lung cancer diagnosed in 2005. This would be an example of:
    a.  Prevalence
    b.  Incidence
    c.  Mean
    d.  Mode

**Answer b.** Incidence is the number of new cases in a certain time frame (usually a year).

Prevalence would be the current number of people with the disease (or trait).

534. In a study of an investigational oral chemotherapy agent for patients who have undergone breast CA surgery, patients were randomly assigned to either the experimental drug or Tamoxifen. The patients were not aware of which drug they were receiving however the physicians were aware. This would be an example of:
    a.  Cohort study
    b.  Retrospective review
    c.  Double blind randomized control trial
    d.  Single blinded randomized control trial

**Answer d.** Because the physicians were aware of whether or not the patients were receiving the drug or placebo, it is only a single blinded randomized control trial.

535. Sensitivity of a test reflects:
    a.  Ability to detect disease
    b.  Ability to say that no disease is present
    c.  Rejecting the null hypothesis when it is true
    d.  Accepting the null hypothesis when it is false

**Answer a.** (see below)

536. Specificity of a test reflects:
   a. Ability to detect disease
   b. Ability to say that no disease is present
   c. Rejecting the null hypothesis when it is true
   d. Accepting the null hypothesis when it is false

**Answer b.** (see below)

537. Type I error reflects:
   a. Ability to detect disease
   b. Ability to say that no disease is present
   c. Rejecting the null hypothesis when it is true
   d. Accepting the null hypothesis when it is false

**Answer c.** (see below)

538. Type II error reflects:
   a. Ability to detect disease
   b. Ability to say that no disease is present
   c. Rejecting the null hypothesis when it is true
   d. Accepting the null hypothesis when it is false

**Answer d.**

**Sensitivity** reflects ability to detect disease.
   = [true positives/(true positive + false negatives)

   With high sensitivity, a negative result means the patient
   is very unlikely to have the disease

   **Specificity** reflects ability to state that no disease is present
   = [true negatives/(true negative + false positives)

237

With high specificity, a positive result means the patient is very likely to have the disease

Type I error – rejects the null hypothesis incorrectly (thinking there is a correlation when in reality there isn't one)

Type II error – accepts the null hypothesis incorrectly (you didn't find a correlation but one actually exists)

The most common reason for a Type II error is low sample size.

539. Power of a test is:
   a. = 1 - probability of Type I error
   b. = 1 - probability of Type II error
   c. = 1 + probability of Type I error
   d. = 1 + probability of Type II error

**Answer b.** The power of a test is the probability of making a right conclusion. A large sample size will increase power (by decreasing the likelihood of a Type II error).

Printed in the United States
124242LV00004B/8/A